How You Learn Is How You Live

Using Nine Ways Of Learning To Transform Your Life

Kay Peterson (Institute For Experiential Learning)

David A. Kolb (Experience Based Learning Systems)

16
EasyRead Large

Copyright Page from the Original Book

How You Learn Is How You Live

Berrett-Koehler Publishers, Inc.
1333 Broadway, Suite 1000
Oakland, CA 94612-1921
Tel: (510) 817-2277, Fax: (510) 817-2278
www.bkconnection.com

Ordering information for print editions
Quantity sales. Special discounts are available on quantity purchases by corporations, associations, and others. For details, contact the "Special Sales Department" at the Berrett-Koehler address above.
Individual sales. Berrett-Koehler publications are available through most bookstores. They can also be ordered directly from Berrett-Koehler: Tel: (800) 929-2929; Fax: (802) 864-7626; www.bkconnection.com
Orders for college textbook/course adoption use. Please contact Berrett-Koehler: Tel: (800) 929-2929; Fax: (802) 864-7626.
Orders by U.S. trade bookstores and wholesalers. Please contact Ingram Publisher Services, Tel: (800) 509-4887; Fax: (800) 838-1149; E-mail: customer.service@ingrampublisherservices.com; or visit www.ingram publisherservices.com/Ordering for details about electronic ordering.

Berrett-Koehler and the BK logo are registered trademarks of Berrett-Koehler Publishers, Inc.

First Edition
Paperback print edition ISBN 978-1-62656-870-9
PDF e-book ISBN 978-1-62656-871-6
IDPF e-book ISBN 978-1-62656-872-3

2017-1

Cover Design: Susan Malikowski/DesignLeaf Studio

Cover Image: Getty Images and 123rf

Interior Illustrations: Getty Images and 123rf

Book Production: Adept Content Solutions

TABLE OF CONTENTS

More Praise for How You Learn Is How You Live i

List of Tables and Figures vi

Foreword vii

Introduction xi

Chapter One: The Learning Way 1

Chapter Two: I Am a Learner 12

Chapter Three: My Learning Style, My Life Path 39

Chapter Four: Building Style Flexibility 85

Chapter Five: Learning Flexibility and the Road Ahead 116

Chapter Six: What's Next? Deliberate Learning for Life 138

Notes 157

References 162

Appendix A: The Kolb Learning Style Inventory 4.0 171

Appendix B: The Style Sheets 176

About the Authors 230

Index 239

More Praise for How You Learn Is How You Live

"As a leadership development coach and continual learner, I loved this book! The authors expertly demonstrate the importance of maximizing our potential through recognizing and developing our personal learning styles. They stress how critical this process is for navigating modern, complex, and ever-changing environments. This book offers assistance through a compelling blend of science, reflective exercises, and real-life examples. I highly recommend it for you, your clients, family, and friends."

—Sandy Carter, MSW, MBA, PhD, Professional Certified Coach

"Many thanks to Kay Peterson and David Kolb for advancing the important discussion of approaching our learning from a place of intention. Their new book, *How You Learn Is How You Live,* is a valuable blend of theory and practice, providing research-based depth to their assertions while also bridging to practical examples that meet the needs of a world that looks for immediate application and results. In my work with leaders, I find that the most successful leaders are those who are open to their own learning. This new work from Peterson and Kolb would be a worthy addition to any leadership library and provides a rich addition to the field of adult learning."

—Mindy Hall, PhD, President and CEO, Peak Development Consulting, LLC

"This is a terrific, practical book about an expanded version of the Kolb learning model. I thought the stories, examples of application, and application tips were practical and at the right degree of detail to help people at all levels and in all functions see how the Kolb learning model can help them grow as individuals and help teams realize their potential."

—Anne Litwin, PhD, President, Anne Litwin and Associates

"*How You Learn Is How You Live* is a practical guide grounded in theoretical research. A useful quick read to identify one's preferred style and provide insight in building human capacity in learning and living."

—Lisa Massarweh, MSN, RN, Director, Kaiser Foundation Hospitals, and Robert Wood Johnson Foundation Executive Nurse Fellow (2006–2009)

"I strongly recommend this book to learners who seek to progress in life, who might be by choice or unexpectedly in transition, or who feel there is more to life than just finding your niche of happiness through pure strengths. Knowing your strengths is imperative, yet having the vision to expand your strengths is inspiring."

—Nancy White, founder and CEO, Workshop AZ

"*How You Learn Is How You Live* portrays a straightforward, clear, and comprehensive approach that helps readers discover and appreciate how their learning style impacts how they experience life. The book is one that you want to reread again and again—something you want to experience again, each time mindfully approaching living and relating to oneself, to others, and to one's contribution to our world's conscious evolution. This is most definitely an impactful book for individuals, for couples, for teams, for organizations—and for the world."

—Philip R. Belzunce, PhD, and Lalei E. Gutierrez, PhD, holistic psychologists, life-relational coaches, and diversity facilitators

"In their book, *How You Learn Is How You Live,* Kay Peterson and David Kolb have gifted us with a highly understandable and eminently practical guidebook on experiential learning and its importance to everything we do in life. In our pressured world of skill shortages and talent gaps, this book is recommended reading for every employer, teacher, guidance counselor, workforce developer, and economic developer concerned about creating the workforce of the future. Learning by doing has eclipsed traditional educational and training and development strategies because it works far better. Learning is a leading source of competitive advantage in today's fast-changing global economy."

—Don Iannone, President, Donald T. Iannone & Associates

"If you have ever wondered how you learn or why others around you may not be adapting and changing, this book will enlighten you. Read it, absorb it, and you will never talk to your children, colleagues, students, patients, or clients the same way!"

—Richard Boyatzis, PhD, Distinguished University Professor, Departments of Psychology, Cognitive Science, and Organizational Behavior, Case Western Reserve University

For Carl, Sarah, Adam, and Alec

for Alice

List of Tables and Figures

Figure 2.1: The Learning Cycle

Figure 2.2: The Experiential Learning Cycle and Regions of the Cerebral Cortex

Figure 3.1: The Nine Learning Styles

Table 3.1: Identifying Your Learning Style

Table 3.2: Communication Preferences by Learning Style

Figure 3.2: Learning Styles as Steps in the Learning Cycle Process

Figure 3.3: Lisa's Team Map of Learning Styles

Table 3.3: Learning Styles to Guide Shared Leadership on Teams

Table 4.1: The Nine Styles of Learning and Their Associated Capabilities

Table 4.2: Questions to Guide Adoption of Learning Styles

Foreword

How You Learn Is How You Live provides a life-enriching formula: become a more attuned learner and you will be better for it. In your career, family, and personal life, a better understanding of the learning process and your learning preferences is the key to a better life.

Kay Peterson and David Kolb provide an engaging look at how to renew your natural ability to learn. Kay and David remind us how exciting and enriching learning can be. By taking what the authors term "the learning way," you can learn more than you ever imagined.

Since the first time I read David Kolb's classic book *Experiential Learning: Experience as the Source of Learning and Development,* I have been hooked on the power of its message: we all learn from experience, and by engaging in the four-phase learning cycle, we can learn almost anything. The ideas and practices associated with learning from experience have informed me professionally and personally. Since being introduced to experiential learning twenty years ago, I have regularly looked for ways to integrate experiential learning into my life, my teaching, and my research. By reading this book and following the learning way, your life will be enriched as well.

If this book marks your first introduction to experiential learning, then you are in for a life-altering experience. The notion that we learn from our experience grew out of the ideas of philosophers and psychologists. David Kolb found a common theme in the diverse thinking on the topic of experiential learning. His work on experiential learning cycle is among the most influential approaches to learning. In colleges, business, and school systems, it is impossible to talk about learning without the mention of David Kolb.

David also introduced the concept of learning style nearly fifty years ago. Learning style describes an individual's unique preference for learning in different ways. As the author of *The Learning Style Inventory*, now in its fourth iteration, David transformed the experiential learning cycle into a hands-on exercise of self-discovery. The learning style inventory has helped hundreds of thousands of individuals realize their potential as learners.

In *How You Learn Is How You Live*, David has partnered with Kay Peterson, an innovative thinker and sought-after consultant. Kay has seen firsthand the power of experiential learning in transforming lives and careers. In her consulting practice, she has implemented organizational and individual change using the underlying values and ideas of experiential learning. Kay's work has proven that experiential learning should be on the agenda of every organizational change effort and on the reading list of anyone looking to enact personal change.

This partnership between Kay and David has resulted in an extraordinary book. As you will see, the book builds on David's work, making it practical and personal. Kay and David provide step-by-step instructions on how to live the ideas of experiential learning.

If you have already discovered Kay and David's work on experiential learning, you will find new insights in this book. Experiential learning is made more accessible than ever. Even the avid follower of experiential learning will find new applications of a tried-and-true formula.

One of the key insights I gained from this book is the power of learning flexibility. Learning flexibility describes our potential to change and adapt. Many of us find change difficult, and this difficulty at change can be traced to our learning style preference. We can get stuck and rely only on a limited set of learning tools. This book describes how to embrace change and move beyond our comfort zone. Luckily, Kay and David provide hands-on exercises and descriptive examples of how to overcome our limits and build upon our strengths by embracing learning flexibility.

Just before reading this book for the first time, I was watching a full moon shining over the Maryland Chesapeake Bay. This wonderful experience was cut short. My thoughts turned to a documentary I had watched earlier in the week about the engineering and psychological challenges of landing the first people on the moon. Experiential learning provides a formula for understanding both the experience of the moon shining and the concepts behind the moon shot. For me, understanding the moon from different perspectives, for example, through my direct experience and through abstract concepts, I am able to see the world in a much richer way. This is the power of experiential learning, to be able to learn from different angles. The ultimate promise of this book is that you, too, will learn how to enrich your life, experience events more deeply, and understand situations with greater clarity.

D. Christopher Kayes,
Professor and Chair, Department of Management,
George Washington University

Introduction

How You Learn Is How You Live is a guide to awakening the power of learning that lies within us—to show how we can increase our capability to learn from experience throughout our lives, in each and every moment. To say that experience is the best teacher is an understatement—it is our only teacher. We are totally enveloped by our experience like a fish is by water. We awake each day to swim in our stream of conscious experience, surrounded once again by the ongoing story of our lives: the trials and tragedies, hopes and dreams, family, friends, and coworkers who make up our world. How we make sense of it all to find meaning, purpose, and direction in our lives is called learning from experience, or experiential learning.

Experiential learning has been studied extensively in the twentieth century by some of the greatest thinkers of our time, including John Dewey, William James, Carl Rogers, and Jean Piaget. David Kolb's Experiential Learning Theory has integrated the ideas of these scholars into a model of learning from experience that is uniquely suited to the learning challenges of the twenty-first century. Since the turn of the century, research studies on the model have more than quadrupled. The current experiential learning theory bibliography includes over four thousand entries from 1971 to 2016. In the field of management alone, a

2013 review of management education research showed that 27 percent of the most cited articles in management education journals were about experiential learning and learning styles.[1]

In over forty-five years of research on the theory by scholars and practitioners all over the world, the principles and practices of experiential learning have been used to develop and deliver programs in K–12 education, undergraduate education, and professional education. In the workplace, training and development activities and executive coaching practices are based on experiential learning concepts. Practices that are based on experiential learning include service learning, problem-based learning, action learning, adventure education, and simulation and gaming. These practices make use of community service, adventure, and gaming to help people become aware of how they process information and apply that awareness to their personal and professional development.

Like the many people who have been introduced to experiential learning through universities or our organizational programs, you can use the approach deliberately to recreate and transform yourself. Experiential learning gives you the tools to take charge of your life. This process can help you improve your performance, learn something new, and achieve your goals. In this book, you will see how understanding the learning process and your own approach to learning is the key to self-transformation and growth.

The first chapter describes the learning way of living, suggesting how giving learning a top priority in your life can bring great satisfaction and fulfillment of your potential. The learning way is an approach to living that requires deep trust in your own experience and a healthy skepticism about information. It demands both the perspective of quiet reflection and a passionate commitment to action in the face of uncertainty. The learning way begins with the awareness that learning is present in every life experience and is an invitation for us to be engaged in each one. We become aware *that* we are learning, *how* we are learning, and—perhaps most importantly—*what* we are learning.

The second chapter, "I Am a Learner," introduces two important first steps on the learning way journey: embracing a learning identity and learning how to learn. The starting point for learning from experience is the belief that you *can* learn and develop from your life experiences. Many people think of themselves as having a fixed identity, believing that they are incapable of changing. At the extreme, if you do not believe that you can learn, you won't.

To thrive on the learning way requires knowing how to learn. The experiential learning cycle is a learning process initiated by a *concrete experience,* which demands *reflective observation* about the experience in a search for meaning that engages *abstract thinking,* leading to a decision to engage in *active experimentation.* This cycle is so simple and natural that people engage in it without being aware that they are learning. It goes on almost effortlessly all the time and is constantly transforming our lives, but we can learn to employ this process actively and take control of our transformation.

Chapter three, "My Learning Style, My Life Path" invites you to examine your own unique approach to learning, your learning style, and its consequences for the path you have taken in your life. You will explore nine ways of living and learning, each of which brings its own joys and satisfactions, presents its own challenges, and brings the learner to a different place. You will probably relate to one way of learning. Other ways will remind you of people you know, friends, family, and coworkers. Understanding your unique way of learning and your learning style will shed light on the path you have taken in your life. It can help you assess your strengths and weaknesses and understand your preferences. Because each of the learning styles has an upside and downside, it's important to identify the learning styles you use and those you avoid. Recognizing the different paths of learning and living that others are on can illuminate the communication problems that arise when someone you know is coming from a different place. It can bring the team synergy that occurs when a partner's strengths cover your weaknesses and vice versa. You can also model yourself after those with styles different from your own and expand your capabilities.

In chapter four, "Building Learning Style Flexibility," you will think of one thing you would like to change in yourself that is most critical for your success—just one, no matter how small. This may be a quality or capability that you would like to acquire. It may be a strength that is overplayed or a weakness that holds you back. This will be a goal that increases your flexibility to use a learning style that is not as familiar to you. This one step will be the beginning of a lifelong quest to increase your ability to use all nine styles of learning. Being aware of your preferences and broadening your comfort zone will help you avoid getting stuck in a rut. Instead, you can create a path of your own by seeing all the possibilities instead of just one style.

Chapter five, "Learning Flexibility and the Road Ahead," shows how, with learning flexibility, you can use the full learning cycle to master whatever challenges you may face on the road ahead: perfecting your special skills, rising to greater responsibility, changing your career, finding work/life balance, or serving a greater purpose.

Finally, chapter six, "What's Next? Deliberate Learning for Life," offers checklists that support the application of the learning way in your life so that you can master the challenges of continuous, lifelong learning.

Chapter One

The Learning Way

For he had learned some of the things that everyman must find out for himself, and he had found out about them as one has to find out, through errors and through trial, through fantasy and delusion, through falsehood and his own damn foolishness, through being mistaken and wrong and an idiot and egotistical and aspiring and hopeful and believing and confused. As he lay there he had gone back over his life, and bit by bit, had extracted from it some of the hard lessons of experience. Each thing he learned was so simple and so obvious once he grasped it, that he wondered why he had not always known it. Altogether, they wove into a kind of leading thread, trailing backward through his past and out into the future. And he thought now, perhaps he could begin to shape his life to mastery, for he felt a sense of new direction deep within him, but whither it would take him he could not say.

Thomas Wolfe

There are many ways to live your life. Each of us is unique, and the life path we choose reflects this uniqueness, amplified for better or worse by luck and circumstance. Stop and think about where you are now at this moment in your life and reflect on the path you have taken to arrive here. You have likely made many good choices with consequences that have brought you happiness and success. There are also probably bad times, bad choices, and unpredictable and uncontrollable events that have challenged you greatly. Through it all you have learned from your experience and have acquired life lessons that guide you on your way. Some of these lessons serve you well, but others, often emotional beliefs born out of disappointment and pain, offer poor advice for living. As Mark Twain advised, "We should be careful to get out of an experience only the wisdom that is in it—and stop there; lest we be like the cat that sits down on a hot stove-lid. She will never sit down on a hot stove-lid again—and that is well; but also she will never sit down on a cold one anymore."

Living each life experience with a learning attitude can help us extract the right lessons from that experience. The learning way is not the easiest way to approach life, but in the long run it is the wisest. Other ways of living tempt us with immediate gratification at our peril. The way of dogma, the way of denial, the way of addiction, the way of submission, and the way of habit; all offer relief from uncertainty and pain at the cost of entrapment on a path that winds out of our control. The learning way requires deliberate effort to create new knowledge in the face of uncertainty and failure, but this process opens the way to new, broader, and deeper horizons of experience.

The learning process itself is intrinsically rewarding and empowering, bringing new avenues of experience and new realms of mastery. The key is to use the *process* of learning as a guide. Oprah Winfrey says it well: "I am a woman in process. I'm just trying like everybody else. I try to take every conflict, every experience, and learn from it. Life is never dull."[1] Oprah's ability to learn from experience cannot be denied: from a young girl in rural Mississippi in the 1950s to talk show host, media entrepreneur, and actress, Oprah keeps learning as she follows her ever-expanding interests.

The lessons we learn from our past experiences are not fixed rules for living but must be open to revision. Each new experience is like no other and must be experienced fully to reap its wisdom. In a life of learning the rules of the game, the rules are always changing, and our process of experiencing is the guiding star.

Experiencing as the Gateway to Learning

Without new experiences there can be no real learning. We only recombine and reiterate what we already know. Opening ourselves to new experiences and living those experiences fully with awareness in the moment is necessary for learning, renewal, and growth. Yet our habits and beliefs tend to engage automatically, turning a new experience into an old pattern of response. Ironically, what we think we know can be the greatest barrier to our learning.

The Nobel Prize–winning psychologist Daniel Kahneman says that we actually have two selves—an experiencing self and a remembered thinking self. Our experiencing self perceives and registers our feelings and reactions to every moment of our lives. For the experiencing self, life is a succession of momentary experiences—happiness, sadness, amazement, boredom, curiosity, love, pain—that exist only in the present and are soon replaced by another feeling. In ancient Theraveda Buddhism this succession of experiences is depicted as a string of pearls. Kahneman similarly thought of this succession of experiences as a string of moments. He took a mathematical approach, calculating the duration of each of these moments:

...each of these moments of psychological present may last up to 3 seconds, suggesting that people experience some 20,000 moments in a waking day, and upwards of 500 million moments in a 70 year life. Each moment can be given a rich multidimensional description.... What happens to these moments? The answer is straightforward: with very few exceptions, they simply disappear. [2]

The remembered thinking self is like the string that holds together the pearls of our experiences. The pearls and the string together form the story of our lives—what we think and feel and who we are. We base all our choices on this life story, but our life story is not always the best basis for decision making. The way that we remember our experiences is very different than the active process of experiencing—our minds create illusions that impact how we remember experiences.

For example, we often give more weight to our most recent experience. This can cause us to remember an event that ended well as a positive event, even if it was filled with painful experiences. A study on vacations found a substantial difference between the vacationers' recalled enjoyment and their actual experienced enjoyment. Their recalled enjoyment, not their actual experienced enjoyment, led them to desire to repeat the vacation. Another study found that people predict they will be happier on their birthday, but their actual experience of happiness is the same as other days. Studies like these emphasize the importance of being in touch with both the experiencing and remembered thinking selves when making life decisions. Being aware of the experiencing process can help us use relevant experiences instead of illusions to guide our decisions.

The balance between the experiencing and remembered thinking selves shifts over the course of our lifetime. As children we are guided primarily by our experiencing process and as a result are spontaneous, authentic, and able to easily embrace contradiction and change. As we grow older our remembered thinking self takes charge. Our experiences are impacted by memories, beliefs, and values that are not always relevant. Carl Rogers argues that the mature adult needs to recapture the child's capacity to experience directly. He describes this as a process of "letting oneself down into the immediacy of what one is experiencing, endeavoring to sense and to clarify all its complex meanings."[3] He explains that adults experience not only the present moment but also their memories of the past and predictions about the future, so they must strive to consciously interpret each experience anew.

Creating Ourselves by Learning

Much of who we are is determined by what we have learned from our life experiences. As we have seen, experiences matter, but we use the meaning we make of them to define ourselves. Our birth brings us into poverty or privilege, yet many have risen from the lowest to the highest rungs of society by choosing to see their conditions as a challenge while many of the most privileged have squandered their riches through indifference. Sometimes learning creates profound transformation in a person's life. By learning, doors can be opened through the barriers of class, race, gender, and ethnic identification. It can open eyes and hearts to the experience of others. It transforms the child's awkward grasp into the surgeon's skilled hand.

Some experiences are thrust upon us; some we create for ourselves. We string these experiences together like pearls to define who we are. Looking forward to the future, we see the pearls are only dreams and distant visions of our future experiences. The experience in *this* present moment is all that actually exists. In the present moment, we fashion a pearl of meaning to remember and choose the next experience ahead. The next experience offers new possibilities for meaning and choice, and on so on in a lifelong process of self-creation and learning.

In some spiritual traditions we humans are thought to be basically asleep, going through life in a semiconscious way, strangely disengaged from our own lives. The learning way is about awakening to attend consciously to our experiences and then to deliberately choose how they influence our beliefs and choices. The spiral of learning from experience—experiencing, reflecting, thinking, and acting—is the process by which we can consciously choose, direct, and control our life.

The Learning Life Force

The learning way is about awakening the learning life force that lies within all of us. It is a power that we share with all living things. The Chilean biologists Humberto Maturana and Francisco Varela in their search for the defining characteristic of life discovered the process of *autopoeisis,* the continual process of remaking ourselves through learning from experience.[4] The basic example of autopoeisis is the biological cell with a nucleus and boundary membrane made up of nucleic acids and proteins, and it happens at every level of a system. The bounded structures of the cell like the nucleus and membrane rely on external energy and molecules to produce the cell components that maintain these. Learning from conscious experience is the highest form of this auto-poetic learning life force. Every human invention and achievement is the result of this process. The great humanistic psychologist, Abraham Maslow, described the process as *"self-actualization"*—the human motivation to fulfill our full potential.[5] Our learning is driven by this desire to get it right, to do better, and to reach our greatest aspirations for ourselves and the world.

We develop and grow as human beings through learning As children we acquire the basic skills we need to survive. In our early adult years we strive to find a specialization that suits our interests and gives us a place to fit in to society. But we are not done growing when we finish our formal education or even when we successfully arrive at the top of a chosen profession. In fact, we continue to grow throughout our life in a predictable pattern of adult development. In much the same way that we expand our understanding of the world from adolescence to adulthood, we can continue to expand our mental, emotional, and relational capabilities to entirely new levels of complexity and flexibility in response to the increasingly demanding world around us. Maturity in life and career should be seen as a process of unfolding rather than a status achieved once. Contemporary adult development theories describe the course of adult life as a process of learning from life challenges that culminates in what is called self-authorship—becoming the creator of one's own life story. Self-authorship describes individuals who see themselves as independent selves who are responsible for their actions and in control of their lives. They trust their experiences and build a belief system around those experiences, developing meaningful relationships and a strong sense of personal identity.

A Life of Moral Purpose

There are some who warn against trusting our experiences to guide our learning and life. They believe that focusing on personal experiences leads to self-absorption and obliviousness to the needs and concerns of others, and they argue that we should follow time-tested moral rules instead. Yet Carl Rogers maintains that our internal process of deep experiencing is a highly developed way of knowing the good, the true, and the beautiful. He believes that we developed this process through centuries of evolution, making it acutely attuned to survival not only of the individual but all of humanity. He argues that our true moral purpose is not to blindly follow the values developed by philosophers, religious and political leaders, or psychologists but rather to connect with our innate sense of morality through deep experiencing.[6] Deep experiencing means paying attention to and learning from our experiences; doing so helps us develop as both individuals and members of communities, benefiting the whole of humanity.

Empathy, the ability to identify with others, is what drives us to act morally with others. Learning through shared experience with others is the foundation of a life with moral purpose. John Dewey describes that purpose "…to learn from life itself and to make the conditions of life such that all will learn in the process of living."[7]

Learning as a Humble Way

To learn requires giving up the certainty that we know something. We must be open to seeing new possibilities. We must recognize that we can only drink from the ocean of experience teacup by teacup and that our previous conceptions must always be tested by new information—we must be humble learners. Being a humble learner does not mean being simple, weak, or insecure. Because the gift of learning is mastery and greater knowledge, as learners we acquire a secure self-confidence and sense of competence. Yet the openness to experience that brings new learning also prevents this self-esteem from becoming arrogance or dogmatism. Humble learners are fully aware of their talents and abilities but also know their limitations. Recognizing that they are always in the process of learning allows them to admit limitations and mistakes and be willing to learn from others.

Chapter Two

I Am a Learner

When I look back on it now, I am so glad that the one thing I had in my life was my belief that everything in life is a learning experience, whether it be positive or negative. If you can see it as a learning experience, you can turn any negative into a positive.

Neve Campbell

I am a learner. True or false? Maybe? Sometimes? How would you answer? Many would answer false. They believe that they have what psychologist Carol Dweck calls a "fixed identity."[1] People are born smart or dumb. The smart ones "get it," and the dumb ones never will. Others aren't sure. They got through school reasonably well and have managed to accomplish many things on the job, but they are not sure this is because of any effort they made to learn. It seemed almost automatic for them. Still others might answer, "Sometimes I am a learner." They may be specialists who can deliberately learn things about their specialty quickly and easily, but when a partner says "Let's take a dance class," they reply, "I can't dance." They adopt a fixed identity outside of their specialty.

The correct answer is true. You are a learner. Learning is almost synonymous with life itself. We share the capacity to learn with all other living things. The process of evolution is a learning process, and as humans we stand at the pinnacle of the capacity to learn. But learning is such a wondrous, powerful, and mysteriously complex process that you may not be aware of it. From the moment you entered the world, you have been learning all the time, and as a baby and young child the speed and power of your learning were enormous. Most of this learning was unconscious, occurring through a simple cycle of learning that James Zull, a biologist and founding director of Case Western Reserve University Center for Innovation in Teaching and Education (UCITE), calls the exploration/mimicry learning process.[2] This cycle uses only a limited part of the brain and the sensory and motor regions without intervening reflection and thinking. The child learns language in this way, mimicking and repeating the sounds of the mother's voice. Through this process, we learn many complex skills from walking, talking, reading, and writing to even more sophisticated expert skills, such as medical diagnosis.

In adults, the process slows somewhat because of fixed habits, skills, and entrenched beliefs. The networks established in our brains by these habits, skills, and beliefs reduce the brain's openness to learning and determine most of our behavior unconsciously and automatically. This is called *"automaticity,"* and research suggests that as much as 90 percent of our behavior is determined in this way.[3] It is little wonder that someone might answer "maybe," not being sure whether they are a learner.

Paradoxically, however, as the frontal regions of our brains mature, we also become capable of what we call full-cycle learning. In addition to simply perceiving and acting, we develop the capacity for critical reflection and conceptual, creative thinking. We develop the ability to take conscious control of our learning, deliberately focusing our learning power on anything we choose. We can critically examine, evaluate, and change habits and beliefs that we acquired automatically through associating with others, and we can improve existing skills and develop new ones.

The First Step—Embracing a Learning Identity

The first step on the learning way is embracing a learning identity—a confidence and belief in your capacity to learn. Many people believe that they are incapable of learning. Learning from experience must start with the belief that learning and developing from life experiences is possible. Most learning requires conscious attention, effort, and time. These activities seem like a waste of time to those who do not believe that they have the ability to learn.

Paulo Freire demonstrated the importance of developing a learning identity in his literacy work with

Brazilian peasant farmers. Freire believed that oppressed individuals absorb society's message that they are unproductive and incapable of learning and develop these negative stereotypes as a fixed identity. So the Brazilian farmers could escape this negative identity, Freire helped them develop critical consciousness through reflection and action.[4] Breaking free of their negative, fixed identity helped the farmers understand that they could analyze and change the political and cultural realities affecting their lives. They formed consciousness-raising, protest, and labor organizations to bring about changes in their conditions. People with a learning identity see themselves as learners, seek out experiences with a learning attitude, and believe in their ability to learn.

Learners approach a difficult challenge with a *mastery response,* persist in the face of obstacles, learn from criticism, and are inspired by and learn from the success of others. In contrast, people with a fixed identity avoid challenges, give up easily, avoid criticism, and feel threatened by the success of others. Not surprisingly, students with a learning identity, regardless of their tested intelligence, are more successful in school than those with a fixed identity.

You can *learn* to consider yourself a learner. Being able to say with confidence, "I am a learner," is not accomplished overnight; a learning identity develops over time. The vast majority of us have elements of both fixed and learning identities. We may feel that we are good at learning some things, like sports, and not good at others, like mathematics. We must learn to overcome characteristics that reinforce a fixed self—such as negative self-talk, avoidance of risk and failure, and being threatened by the successes of others—and build those that reinforce a learning self—such as trusting one's ability to learn from experience, seeking new experiences and challenges, persistence, learning from mistakes, and using others' success as a source of learning.

The Second Step—Learning How to Learn

To thrive on the learning way requires knowing *how* to learn. Let's examine this process more closely in a common experience that we all share: meeting someone new.

Cheryl is attending a reception for new employees at her company. She enters the room and walks over to a smiling well-dressed woman near the door. "Hi, my name is Cheryl Johnson, and I'm in accounting. Welcome to TLC!" The woman responds by introducing herself, saying that she has just started working in the president's office.

Cheryl says, "I just love your dress! It looks so great on you. Where did you get it?"

The woman, beaming, says, "thanks," and a lively conversation continues for some time before Cheryl moves on to greet others.

Later that evening at dinner with her husband, Cheryl says, "I met the new hire in the president's office at the reception, and she was wearing a dress that would be perfect for our trip this weekend. It's on sale at Ann Taylor."

"Did—what did you say her name was—say how much it cost?" he asks.

Cheryl suddenly realizes that she has no recollection of the woman's name. "You know I am no good at remembering names."

"I know," he chuckles.

Nearly everyone has had an experience like Cheryl's of failing to remember someone's name after meeting them. A bad memory for names is the most common explanation people come up with. There are a number of reasons why Cheryl might not have learned the new employee's name, and most of them are more probable than "a bad memory." The most likely one in this case is that Cheryl didn't hear or take in the employee's name in the first place. Having just entered the room, she may have been still thinking about work or feeling nervous about meeting a bunch of new people. People often meet in a distracting environment or with feelings of uneasiness without giving the exchange of their names full attention.

Cheryl also may have been focused on learning something else from the experience, having spied a dress that she liked. The conversation was, after all, a successful learning experience from her point of view. Unfortunately, however, it appears that she also learned something more consequential from the experience—that she is no good at remembering names. Her husband's comment unintentionally reinforced her fixed, nonlearning view of herself as someone who has a bad memory for names.

If you, like Cheryl, have trouble remembering names, adopt a learning attitude and apply the experiential learning cycle to the problem. The experiential learning cycle is a four-step learning process that is applied several times in every interaction: *experience, reflect, think,* and *act.* When first meeting a new person, attend to the *experience* of being with that person and hearing his or her name. Get a feeling for the person. If you miss the name, slow down the interaction and ask the person to repeat it. Don't be embarrassed. Most people are flattered that you care to get their name right. Next, *reflect* on your experience of the person and what his or her name means to you. *Think* by connecting your reflections to related concepts you may have, such as, "This Betty is different than the other Bettys I know. My sister's name is Betty, too. The staff members in the president's office are now Betty, Sarah, and Kyle." Finally, *act.* Use the person's name several times in your conversation and in later conversations with others.

Let's take a closer look at the learning cycle and how we learn from our life experiences with another example. Imagine driving to work on a rainy day in your aging Ford, lost in thought, planning your day's activities. You flip on the windshield wipers and find they are not working. You suddenly are brought back to the immediate situation, searching for a solution, checking to see if you can see OK in the light rain. The little tinge of anxiety you feel subsides, and your attention shifts to the worn and dirty seats, the rough hesitation when you accelerate, and the beat-up look of your car. You begin to imagine, "Maybe it's time to buy a new car." You become aware of all the fancy cars surrounding you on the freeway and wonder, "Can I afford it?" You spend the rest of your drive to work dreaming of the possibilities. At your desk, you search Consumer Reports online for the best options and begin researching alternatives in earnest. That weekend, you visit local dealers, take a couple of test drives, and finally trade the old Ford in for a new one.

This simple story describes a process of learning from experience that follows what we call the experiential learning cycle (see Figure 2.1). The learning process was initiated by the *concrete experience* of windshield wipers failing to turn on. This unexpected event demanded conscious attention and led to *reflective observation* about the experience, beginning with a check to see if emergency action was necessary and then progressing to broader ideas about the implications of the malfunction and the possibilities of buying a new car. The thought of buying a new car engaged *abstract thinking*— in this case, researching models of cars and analyzing the costs and benefits of each one. This resulted in deciding to engage in *active experimentation:* exploring auto dealers, taking test drives, and ultimately deciding to buy. This cycle is so simple and natural that we engage in it without even being aware that we are learning. It goes on almost effortlessly all the time, and it is constantly transforming our lives; that new car might save your life, or at least make it more enjoyable and less stressful.

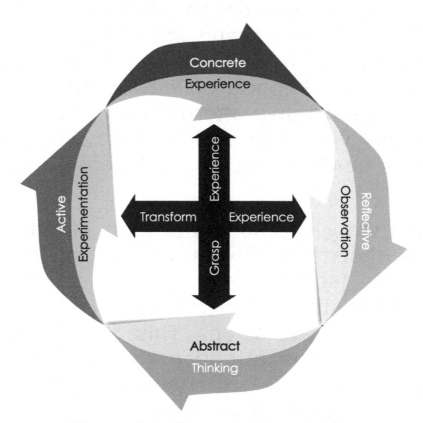

Figure 2.1 The Learning Cycle.

Source: Adapted from Kolb, D.A. (2015). Experiential Learning: Experience as the Source of Learning and Development. 2nd Edition Upper Saddle River, NJ: Pearson Education.

To understand how the learning cycle transforms our lives, let's take a closer look at Figure 2.1. Notice that the four steps of the learning cycle occupy two dimensions. These dimensions represent two different ways in which we understand the world. Our knowledge of the old Ford comes from directly *experiencing* the car and its aging parts. On the other hand, our knowledge of the car world comes from *thinking* about the features and prices of different cars on the market and interpreting those facts. Experiencing and thinking are different ways of knowing the world. Experiencing is direct and specific to the context we are in, while abstract thinking is generalized and applicable in all contexts. Neither experiencing nor thinking can function alone—we must use both dimensions and all four steps of the cycle in order to learn effectively.

The second dimension of the learning cycle includes reflective observation and active experimentation, the two ways we transform and connect our experiences and thoughts. We connect our experience of the wiper breakdown to our knowledge about possible new car options by *reflecting* about the meaning and implications of our experience. We transform our abstract thinking about the car world into the decision to buy a car by *acting* on our research and testing out options.

Reflecting and acting are ways of transforming experiences and thoughts that require one another to produce learning. When we reflect without acting, we have trouble accomplishing change and may become overwhelmed with possibilities, but when we act without reflecting on the consequences of our actions, our decisions become aimless and random.

Using all of the four steps of the learning cycle leads to full-cycle learning. Full-cycle learners touch all the bases—experiencing, reflecting, thinking, and acting—in an ongoing process that adapts to what is being learned and in what environment.

James Zull explores the neurological basis of experiential learning in his 2002 book, *The Art of Changing the Brain: Enriching Teaching by Exploring the Biology of Learning.* His basic idea is that knowledge resides in networks of neurons in the neocortex that are constructed through learning from experience. Learning is a process that builds on the foundation of each individual's neuronal structure; every learner is unique and will interpret experiences differently. Learning from experience results in modification, growth, and pruning of neurons, synapses, and neuronal networks. Thus learning physically changes the brain.

Zull saw a link between experiential learning and the structure of the brain and suggested that understanding the brain's structure can enrich our understanding of the experiential learning process. This relationship between the learning cycle and the process of brain functioning is shown in Figure 2.2. The figure illustrates that concrete experiences are processed in the sensory cortex, reflective observation involves the temporal integrative cortex, the creation of new abstract concepts occurs in the frontal integrative cortex, and active testing involves the motor cortex. In other words, the learning cycle mirrors the structure of the brain.[5]

Zull proposed that these regions of the brain were heavily but not exclusively involved in the modes of the learning cycle He describes a cognitive neuroscience experiment showing that monkeys can distinguish cats from dogs and, more importantly, in doing so, they followed the sequence of the learning cycle in the brain regions his theory predicted. First, the sensory cortex of each monkey was activated by its direct experience: perceiving cat and dog images. Then its temporal cortex was stimulated as it reflected on those images, comparing the images it was being shown to previous images it remembered. Next, its frontal integrative cortex was active as it thought about each image, deciding whether the image represented a cat or dog. Finally, its motor brain was active when the monkey tested its judgment by pressing a red button or a green button, depending on whether it thought the image represented a dog or a cat.

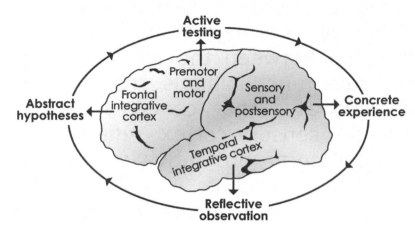

Figure 2.2 The Experiential Learning Cycle and Regions of the Cerebral Cortex.

Source: Zull, J. The Art of Changing the Brain. Sterling, VA: Stylus, 2002. Reprinted with permission of the author.

You may notice that this idea of learning from experience is different from the idea of learning that you may have experienced in school. The most important aspect of the learning cycle is that it describes the learning process as an ongoing spiral that leads us to new experiences. This is quite different from the model of learning where information transferred from the teacher to the learner is meant to be memorized for later recall and testing. In the linear model, the learner is a passive recipient of information, whereas in the cycle of learning, learners receive information through experiences, reflect on it, think about it abstractly to connect it with related information, and then use it to take action. Here, we are both receivers of information and creators of information.

Thus, the second step on the learning way, after embracing a learning identity, is to use the learning cycle as a guide to choose your life path and shape your destiny. We are shaped by our experiences, but through learning we have the transformative power to choose the experiences that are most fulfilling in order to shape our destiny. As infants, we are born with the potential to be anything. Our brains, with as many neurons as stars in the Milky Way, are largely undeveloped. With our first breath, we begin to learn and build neuronal connections, establishing patterns of perception and action as we explore our environment. Gradually, these connections will determine and shape our life path, defining a road ahead but leaving behind many "roads not taken." We learn a language, but don't learn others. We develop some skills and interests and avoid others. Through our lifetime, our one hundred billion neurons will be programmed by countless trips through the learning cycle, with over one thousand trillion connections defining our hopes and dreams, who we are, and what we can be. As adults who believe in ourselves as learners, we have the power to control these choices through deliberate learning from our life experiences.

Using the Learning Cycle for a Life of Learning

In the learning way, the definition of learning expands from what happens in the classroom to what happens in life. The way we learn is actually the way we live. The learning cycle applies not only to formal learning situations but also to day-to-day problem-solving, decision-making, creating, and innovating. The learning cycle can even guide us through personal interactions, meetings, telephone calls, and teamwork. We can approach every situation as a learning opportunity and benefit from using the learning cycle as a guide.

The following story about Amelia illustrates how the learning cycle can guide decision-making for maximum effectiveness. Amelia had been offered a programmer position with a new IT company and needed to compare this offer with staying in her current role at an established company. Amelia started by focusing on the experience of being offered a new job. She tuned in to how she felt during the interview and what her emotions and intuition were telling her about the role, the organization, and her new colleagues. Amelia then reflected to inquire more deeply about her feelings and connect them with the information she had about the position and the company. She sought others' opinions and looked from many perspectives to examine the upsides and downsides of making the change. Here, Amelia took time to test her assumptions, making sure that she examined the ramifications of all of the information she possessed. Next, Amelia stepped back to use abstract thinking. She considered the benefits of this offer compared to staying at her job by concentrating on the facts and quantitative data that were available to her. During this phase, Amelia judged that she was missing an important piece of information about the amount of travel that would be required in the new job. When she was ready to act, rather than committing to a firm decision, Amelia called the interviewer to inquire about the missing information she needed to make the decision. Once she received it, she realized that she needed to cycle through the process again, adding this new information into the mix. Amelia recognized that some parts of the cycle were easier for her than others, but she was satisfied that this process of decision-making included her feelings, perceptions, thoughts, and actions. She knew the outcome would reflect this holistic perspective.

The learning cycle can be used to learn new skills or apply existing skills to new situations. For instance, Alex used the learning cycle to learn how to develop clients in his new role as a partner in a law firm. For eight years as an associate, Alex had worked fifty- to sixty-hour weeks at his firm in order to exceed the expectations of the partners who would decide if he would be one of the few attorneys they would select to join them as owners of the firm. Finally, last year, Alex was voted in as an equity partner. As a part-owner, Alex would share in the profits of the firm, and he would also be required to bring in his own clients. Nothing in Alex's past had prepared him to build new business with clients—or so he thought. In fact, as an associate, he rarely interacted with clients, and he preferred it that way. Alex loved the practice of law, but now that he needed to learn the business of law too, he thought, "I did not become a lawyer to be a salesman."

Alex had a breakthrough when his firm sponsored a professional development program that focused on building a client base. Here, using the learning cycle, Alex began to view client development as a learning challenge that he could master, not something to be avoided. In the experiencing mode, he would need to build authentic relationships so that he could build trust with prospective customers, which is the essence of creating a positive client experience. To do that, he would need to learn about their values, perspectives, and ideal outcomes. In reflection, Alex spent time mulling over relationships he had already built with partners in the firm. He realized that he had some experience on which to draw because he had developed internal clients with partners who had sent work his way. He also thought about the many networks of acquaintances he had developed over the years. Might they be interested in his services?

Alex progressed to abstract thinking by drawing on something he knew well: his ability to synthesize lots of information. He created contact lists of prospective clients, placing them on several lists according to how well he knew them. Here, Alex focused on his own expertise, too, by staying on the forefront of his field and providing exceptional value to existing clients. He thought of the many ways he could provide information to enhance his reputation by publishing articles and blogs and speaking to interest groups and community organizations. Next, Alex devised a plan to give his client development efforts the same energy he gave to his legal work. He firmly committed to allocating one hour per week to client development activities. This consisted primarily of reaching out by email and phone and having a monthly lunch date with a strategic prospect. Finally, Alex enlisted the acting mode of the learning cycle when he met with people and, when appropriate, asked for their business. Alex admitted that this part of the cycle would be the most difficult for him because it was the most unfamiliar. He would need to practice on some low-risk prospects before he built his confidence to execute this portion of the process on large and complex clients, but Alex was convinced that he could learn.

Six months later, Alex was finding the most success in the *experiencing, reflecting,* and *thinking* parts of the learning cycle. For instance, he was enjoying reconnecting with past acquaintances and getting to know people in his network. Although asking people to hire him as their attorney was still uncomfortable for him, Alex was partnering with more senior colleagues who became role models during prospective client meetings. One colleague in particular seemed to have a softer style that Alex liked, and he noticed that he did not feel nervous when this colleague asked for business at all. Alex was learning from experience in many ways.

What if Alex had completely missed one portion of the learning cycle as he approached the client development process, or what if he focused on only one step? Had he ignored the experiencing step, he might have dismissed the power of building relationships. But focusing exclusively on experiencing would not yield results either, because Alex might come up with new ideas without taking action. Skipping the reflecting step might have left Alex without the information he needed on his clients or on his legal specialty, but overfocusing on this step could have left him in analysis paralysis. If Alex had skipped abstract thinking, he would have omitted the very important step of setting goals and measuring himself against a standard. Getting stuck in abstract thinking, however, would have left him recreating the same outcome time and again with no new information to refine it, or he might have aimed for the wrong goal entirely. Finally, skipping the acting step would result in Alex never taking his intention into the outside world of real client development efforts. All the careful planning in the world would have been of no value if Alex had not executed the plan. Yet, if Alex only asked for business without planning or backing up his plans with substance, he would have quickly lost the impeccable reputation he was trying to develop.

Amelia and Alex used the learning cycle to address challenges they faced at work, but the cycle can be used even for household duties as well. For example, Jane found the learning cycle helpful for grocery shopping. When she considered her grocery shopping process, she realized that she was favoring the experiencing and acting steps of the learning cycle and avoiding the reflecting and abstract thinking steps. She said,

I prefer to go shopping when I am down to brass tacks in the fridge. I have a general, big idea of what I need, but I rarely make out a shopping list or scan for existing ingredients required to make specific recipes. When I enter the store—usually when I am hungry—I love the sensory overload of the produce section. The colors, smells, and textures of the fruits and vegetables make me imagine that I will actually consume all that I buy. Occasionally, I feel like a smart shopper who compares pricing, but typically I have preferred brands that are my "go-to" standards. It's only after I get home—usually around 6PM—when I am starting to make dinner that I find a missing ingredient that is central to the dinner I planned to make. Without fail, I vow to start a grocery list for next time, yet I don't make one.

What's missing in Jane's approach? She could use reflecting to identify the items that she wants and needs and then create a list of all the ingredients she needs for those meals. Then, Jane could use thinking to research where she will find the best prices to determine if what she has on her list falls within her budget and to commit to a routine time to shop when she is not hungry so that she can shop using a more practical approach.

In contrast to Jane, who relied heavily on the experiencing step, many professionals tend to neglect experiencing—especially those who specialize in science, math, engineering, or technology. Many of these individuals rely heavily on quantitative problem solving and may not realize the importance of direct experience. One example of a professional like this is Claire, a managing partner of a large law firm. Claire had the opportunity to participate in a leadership development program where she role-played a real client situation to receive feedback on her approach. The client assigned to her in the role-play was grappling with a decision regarding whether to accept a generous offer from a competitor to buy his privately held business. This client had started the business from scratch some fifty years earlier and had built it into a thriving manufacturing facility that employed several family members and many people in the local community.

Claire listened intently to all the facts and proceeded to give the man all the correct advice on structuring the complex deal to his greatest advantage. During the feedback, the client simply shook his head and said, "You got all the numbers right, and your technical expertise was impeccable, but that didn't matter because you didn't pick up on what was important to me. All I needed was for you to appreciate what an emotional decision this has been. It has been the most difficult decision of my life, and I just needed someone to acknowledge that there is more involved than the money." While Claire had provided rock-solid technical advice, she had not been receptive to the impact that emotions were playing in the client's experience because she was not connected to her own emotions.

The Third Step—Discovering Your Learning Style

The next chapter is focused on step three in the learning way: discovering your unique learning style. As you can see in the examples above, few of us are automatically able to manage all parts of the learning cycle with equal ease and flexibility.

We find a unique approach that works, and we continue to hone this preference over time until it becomes a stable guiding force. Understanding our own approach to this process provides a breakthrough in self-awareness. It illustrates which part of the process we favor and which we currently underuse or avoid.

Learning Cycle Checklist for Action

Use the following checklist to make sure you remember and use the learning cycle:

- Create a map of the learning cycle: experiencing, reflecting, thinking, and acting.

- Monitor the way you move around the cycle, noticing which modes are more comfortable and which you avoid or underutilize.

Practice Using the Learning Cycle

Practice navigating the learning cycle. By taking a few minutes to experience going around the learning cycle for yourself, you can see how it works for you in transforming experience into learning. First read through the steps below. Take time to complete each before moving on to the next one.

1. **Create a learning space.** First you need to make a quiet space for yourself to focus on the exercise without distraction. Get physically comfortable and relaxed. Be aware of all that your mind is preoccupied with and consciously set all of those thoughts aside for a few minutes. You can come back to them when you are done.

2. **Focus on an immediate experience.** Let an experience emerge in the space you have made. For instance, you may notice a sensation or feeling in your body. Focus on it and tune in.

Resist the temptation to put those feelings into words. Try to experience the sensations and feelings as vividly as possible. Take enough time for this so that distractions don't interfere with what you are now feeling.

3. **Move to reflection.** Sit back and review what you experienced in the last few moments. Become detached and think of yourself as an observer looking and listening to what you just went through. Don't try to explain the experience at this point. The goal is just to take it in and replay it in your mind as vividly as possible.

4. **Conceptualize the experience.** Now replay your reflections again and try to make sense of them. What is your interpretation of what you were feeling and experiencing? Try to create a concept, word, or idea that summarizes the various aspects of your experience.

5. **Move to action.** What action can you take as a result? Actions can be big or small. You may want to tell someone about what you just went through and get his or her perspective. Your experience may have provided a new insight that makes you want to try a new approach, ask a question, or do something that will move you toward a goal.

6. **The cycle begins again.** Your action will create new experiences and feelings. These may be a little more focused than in the first cycle. You

may want to repeat the above steps again or put it aside for later.

Reflections on Using the Learning Cycle:

You may find it helpful to journal about your use of the learning cycle. Below, you will find prompts for your reflections.

- Describe a recent situation in which you were successful and map the sequence of events (internal and external) on the learning cycle.

- Think of a recent situation in which you were not as successful as you would have liked. Map the events on the learning cycle. Were any steps missing? How might you have benefited from using the learning cycle as your guide?

- Describe a peak moment in your life. Describe how you moved through the learning cycle. Write about how the event unfolded in terms of what occurred during each part of the cycle.

- Pick a theme that is important to you. Create a project or an art piece based on this theme. This can be a poem, sculpture, song, dance, drawing, game, or any kind of creative response. Use the learning cycle to guide you through the process of creation, making changes along the way and being aware that the process is more important than the end product. Reflect on the process and be aware of how the process required you to use the learning cycle. Notice the part of the process that were most comfortable.

Chapter Three

My Learning Style, My Life Path

There is a vitality, a life force, an energy, a quickening, that is translated through you into action, and because there is only one of you in all time, this expression is unique, and if you block it, it will never exist through any other medium and will be lost.

Martha Graham

In this chapter you will examine your unique learning style and its consequences for the path you have taken in your life. You will explore nine different ways of learning, each of which brings its own joys and satisfactions, presents its own challenges, and leads to a different place. You will probably find that one of these ways of learning feels familiar to you, while others will remind you of people you know. Understanding your learning style can help you assess your strengths and weaknesses and understand your preferences. Recognizing the various learning styles can illuminate the communication problems that arise when someone you know is "coming from a different place." Appreciating the differences between learning styles can strengthen and balance your relationships within organizations, teams, and families as you discover how your weaknesses are covered by another's strengths and vice versa. You can also embrace learning styles different from your own and expand your capabilities. Together, the nine learning styles present a complete portrait of your total potential. Just as each step in the learning cycle represents partial capabilities of the whole process, the nine learning styles also represent parts of a whole person. In total, the nine learning styles give you access to capabilities that are broad enough to successfully manage any situation and to learn from it.

Learning Style: Your Way of Using the Learning Cycle

Your learning style is your dynamic way of navigating the learning cycle, a way that emphasizes some parts of the learning cycle of experiencing, reflecting, thinking, and acting over others. It also describes the way you approach life in general. Do you prefer to immediately rely on your feelings or stand back to think? Do you tend to watch and listen to others or immediately move to action? Since the cycle contains pairs of opposites—experiencing and thinking, reflecting and acting—few people find that they are automatically able to manage all these ways of learning with equal ease and flexibility. After all, how can you think and feel at the same time? How can you watch and act simultaneously? The way you navigate the learning cycle—where you enter and where you prefer to dwell—determines your learning style.

Your learning style is not a fixed personality trait; it's more like a steady state. Popular psychology promotes a tendency toward essentialism in our descriptions of others and ourselves. According to this view one is in their essence an introvert or extrovert. This outmoded view promotes both a fixed personal identity and a stereotype of others. It is a shallow portrait of the multidimensional uniqueness of every individual, a portrait that is immune to change, learning, and development.

Figure 3.1 The Nine Learning Styles.

Source: Adapted from David A. Kolb PhD and Alice Kolb PhD. The Kolb Learning Style Inventory 4.0. Experience Based Learning Systems, Inc. 2016.

You will notice that the name of each learning style is a gerund: that is, a verb that functions as noun. This emphasizes the in-process nature of a style as opposed to a static trait. Instead of characterizing someone as a thinker, we say he or she has a Thinking learning style. Although people with a Thinking style may prefer the thinking step of the learning cycle, they are capable of using other learning styles, too.

The Kolb Learning Style Inventory

The Kolb Learning Style Inventory 4.0 (KLSI 4.0) defines the nine learning styles. The KLSI 4.0 is the latest of six versions originally developed by David A. Kolb as a self-assessment and a tool for validating Experiential Learning Theory. The KLSI has been continuously refined over forty years and is the basis for the nine learning styles illustrated in Figure 3.1. For more information on the KLSI 4.0, including how to take the assessment online, please see Appendix A. You can also use the quiz in Table 3.1 to determine your learning style.

Most people have a strong preference for one learning style and use backup styles in their repertoire. They also find that they avoid or underutilize certain styles.

In the quiz, rank the style that seems most like you (9 or <9) and the styles that are least like you (1 or >1).

Learning Style Description and Strength	Key Skills	Rank 1–9
Experiencing		
When using the Experiencing style, you are engaged, connected, warm, and intuitive. You excel in teamwork and establish trusting relationships with others. You are comfortable with emotional expression, and you manage emotions well, even in stressful situations.	▪ Establishing trusting relationships ▪ Being involved and engaged ▪ Connecting personally when communicating ▪ Being comfortable with emotional expression	
Imagining		
When using the Imagining style, you are caring, trusting, empathetic, and creative. You demonstrate self-awareness and empathy for others. You are comfortable in ambiguous situations, and you enjoy helping others, generating new ideas, and creating a vision for the future.	▪ Generating new ideas ▪ Demonstrating empathy for others ▪ Seeking others' opinions ▪ Imagining new possibilities	
Reflecting		
When using the Reflecting style, you are patient, careful, and reserved, allowing others to take center stage. You listen with an open mind and gather information from a variety of sources. You are able to view issues from many perspectives and identify underlying problems and issues.	▪ Listening with an open mind ▪ Gathering information from a variety of sources ▪ Identifying underlying problems and issues ▪ Viewing issues from many perspectives	

Learning Style Description and Strength	Key Skills	Rank 1–9
Analyzing		
When using the Analyzing style, you are structured, methodical, and precise. You plan ahead to minimize mistakes, integrate information to get the full picture, and use critical thinking to understand situations. You are methodical as you analyze details and data.	▪ Planning ahead to minimize mistakes ▪ Organizing information to get the full picture ▪ Analyzing data ▪ Using theories and models to explain issues	
Thinking		
When using the Thinking style, you are skeptical, structured, linear, and controlled. You use quantitative tools to analyze problems and frame arguments with logic. You know how to communicate ideas effectively and make independent judgments.	▪ Using data to analyze solutions ▪ Framing arguments with logic ▪ Using critical thinking for objective communication ▪ Making independent judgments	
Deciding		
When using the Deciding style, you are realistic, accountable, and direct. You find practical solutions to problems, and set performance goals. You are able to commit to one focus.	▪ Finding practical solutions to problems ▪ Committing to a goal ▪ Making decisions and solving problems ▪ Taking a stand, even on controversial issues	

Learning Style Description and Strength	Key Skills	Rank 1–9
Acting		
When using the Acting style, you are on-time, assertive, achievement oriented, and courageous. You commit to goals and objectives and find ways to accomplish them under a deadline. You are able to implement plans with limited resources.	■ Meeting time deadlines ■ Finding ways to make things happen ■ Taking goal-oriented action to achieve results ■ Implementing plans with limited resources	
Initiating		
When using the Initiating style, you are outgoing, spontaneous, and able to shrug off losses or "failure" in favor of trying again. You actively seize opportunities and participate without holding back.	■ Flexibly adapting to changing conditions ■ Influencing and motivating others ■ Recognizing new opportunities ■ Bouncing back from failure	
Balancing		
When using the Balancing style, you identify blind spots in a situation and bridge differences between people. You are resourceful and can adapt to shifting priorities.	■ Identifying the blind spots in a whole situation ■ Bridging differences between people ■ Adapting to shifting priorities ■ Displaying resourcefulness	

Table 3.1 Identifying Your Learning Style

Read through the full descriptions of the nine learning styles to identify your preferred approach, your backup styles and the styles you avoid. As you spiral around the learning cycle, you tend to start with your preferred approach and default to it when you are on automatic pilot or under stress. You can read more about the capabilities and applications of each style in Appendix B.

The Nine Learning Styles of the KLSI 4.0

The Experiencing style. In the Experiencing style, individuals emphasize primarily the feeling capabilities of the learning cycle while balancing Acting and Reflecting. They pay the least attention to the Thinking style. Their greatest strengths are in their ability to deeply involve themselves in concrete experiences while being equally comfortable in the outer world of action and the inner world of reflection. They are particularly adept in building and being in relationships.

People who prefer the Experiencing style are insightful, empathetic, warm, and engaging. They are comfortable with emotional expression, know how to be mindful and present, use all of their five senses, and trust their intuition. If someone overuses the Experiencing style, he dreads the word *objectivity,* may become overly emotional, and calls exclusively on his inner circle of friends rather than seeking out critical evaluation.

Sophia, a chief nursing officer, is an example of someone who prefers the Experiencing style. She says,

I always wanted to be a nurse—I had a way of connecting with people that seemed to be healing.

Now that I have a leadership position, I find that I focus on relationships with my staff just like I did with my patients. I use a team approach to build trust and generate rich conversation so that we can learn about and from each other. How do I make the tough decisions that this role demands? I often use anecdotal information coupled with my intuition and then back it up with data later.

The Imagining style. In the Imagining style, people contemplate experiences and consider a range of possible solutions to create meaning from them. They take in information through Experiencing and process it by Reflecting, paying the least attention to Deciding. Their general approach to situations is to observe rather than take action. People who prefer the Imagining style seek novelty, diversity, and the big picture of what might be possible. They enjoy situations that call for generating a wide range of feelings and ideas, such as brainstorming sessions. They prefer to leave things open; therefore, they can tolerate ambiguity and loose ends in favor of the possibility of finding something better. They are imaginative, sensitive to feelings, have broad cultural interests, and like to gather information.

Those who prefer the Imagining style tend to be caring, trusting, empathetic, and creative. They like personalized attention and working in groups. The Imagining style is inclusive, inviting others in and facilitating situations to meet the needs of others. If someone overuses the Imagining style, she dreads the word *choose,* may be indiscriminate, and may undervalue the practical results of reaching a goal.

Liam, an organizational development manager, prefers the Imagining style. He says,

I am a big-picture person. In fact, I often think I am standing on the balcony while others are on the dance floor. From there, I can detect patterns of emotional energy and patterns in events, relationships, and interactions—I find that I am always connecting the dots to anticipate the outcomes of any potential decision and immediately trying to improve upon it. People say that I see new possibilities that they could not imagine. I'd say that my strong suit in organizational development is interviewing stakeholders at the beginning of any project, getting everyone's opinion and perspective about what needs to change. They seem to know I am an empathetic person and want to help.

The Reflecting style. People who prefer the Reflecting style take in information either by Experiencing or Thinking and process it by Reflecting. They postpone Acting until they are sure of success. People who prefer Reflecting dive into feelings and concepts, equally comfortable in reflection on experiencing (feelings) and thinking (concepts). They mull over information from every angle, pause to watch and listen, and then consider multiple perspectives to be thorough. They learn by combining the abilities of creative idea generation and putting ideas into concise, logical form. As a result, they have a rich and intuitive understanding of matters of importance to them. In the Reflecting style, people enjoy exploring "why" things are the way they are, but they also thrive in uncovering "what" makes the world turn. Those who prefer Reflecting style are patient and quiet, allowing others to take center stage. If someone overuses the Reflecting style, he dreads the word *urgent,* may miss opportunities from trying to get things just right, and may hold back from speaking up.

Jacob, a human resources manager, explains his preferred Reflecting style:

I have always loved taking classes to keep up with the deepest thinking in HR. After any continuing education program, I read all I can on the topic to understand the theory behind it and to figure out how it might impact our employees from every perspective. Then, I still take my time to make decisions about implementing new programs. In fact, I have found that if I partner with a colleague who is more comfortable in the Acting style than I am, she nudges me—I am very deliberate, so this helps to get programs rolled out a little faster. She is actually a good role model for me; I pick up tricks that I can practice in my head before I try them on the job. I especially wish that I could speak up at group meetings like she does. Yet, I find that on those occasions when I do offer my opinion, people really listen to me.

The Analyzing style. In the Analyzing style individuals organize and systematize abundant information into a meaningful whole. They learn primarily through a combination of Thinking and Reflecting, paying the least attention to Initiating. They carefully examine all the details and plan in order to minimize mistakes. Generally they find it more important that a theory have elegance and logical soundness than practical value.

Those who prefer the Analyzing style are structured, methodical, controlled, and precise. Because they place less emphasis on feeling and acting in their style, they may prefer to work alone. They do not make quick decisions; instead, they prefer to think things through. If someone overuses the Analyzing style, she dreads situations that call for *improvisation,* prefers to micromanage projects, and occasionally misses the forest for the trees.

Xia, a financial planner who prefers the Analyzing style says,

More than anything, I get satisfaction by gathering and organizing information—lots of information—then making sense of it so my clients can be sure I've done the research. It's like solving a huge puzzle that seems unsolvable to others. Honestly, I prefer to work alone more than in groups so I can stick to the processes I know are reliable over time. I have always been able to figure things our on my own, especially where numbers and data are concerned. Clients seem to appreciate the way I am able to put all the information into a logical format so that they can make investment decisions. I am able to explain things well to them, especially if it's just one on one or in a small group.

The Thinking style. Individuals who prefer the Thinking style prefer logical analysis and abstract reasoning. They balance Reflecting and Acting, avoiding Experiencing. They are deep thinkers who are able to develop a particular concept or idea and deductively evaluate its validity and practicality by testing it in the real world. They can draw on both the rich inner world of reflection and abstraction and the outer world of action. They thrive on creating conceptual models that can be applied or generalized to other situations.

Those who prefer the Thinking style calculate cost-benefit analysis, rely on contingency flow charts, and look for weakness and inconsistencies in others' work. Because they place little emphasis on feeling in their style, they value being logical and unemotional. They may be uncomfortable with personal relationships and prefer working alone. These individuals are skeptical, structured, linear, and controlled. If someone overuses the Thinking style, he dreads the word *emotional,* may be a loner, or live dispassionately.

Olivia, a financial analyst, prefers the Thinking style. She says,

I am good at what I do—solving problems and predicting outcomes with numbers. I like things to be logical and consistent, and I have to take my time to be certain that I am accurate on my conclusions. To do this, I need to know what outcome is expected from my work and who will be judging it. Once I have a clear framework, I can close my door, take my time, and find all the potential problems lurking beneath the surface of the data. I am proud of my record with the company—no one beats my record with precision in reaching independent judgments. However, if I have to rush, I can get stuck between developing alternatives and making a decision, probably because I am so attached to the Thinking style. Maybe that's the reason that I use "to-do" lists for everything.

The Deciding style. In the Deciding style, people choose a single course of action to solve problems and achieve practical results. They emphasize Thinking and Acting in learning situations, paying the least attention to Imagining. They like to solve problems and make decisions based on finding logical solutions to issues, theories, or problems. In this style, individuals prefer dealing with technical tasks and problems than with social and interpersonal issues.

Those who prefer the Deciding style focus, commit, measure progress toward goals, and drive efficiency. They tend to be realistic, accountable, and direct. These individuals are self-improvement wizards if they see the need to change. If someone overuses the

Deciding style, she dreads the word *brainstorm* and may hold disdain for ambiguity and a lack of focus.

Pierre, a lawyer, describes his preference for the Deciding style:

My clients appreciate the fact that I am always after practical results for them; I keep the bottom line in mind. To do this, I have to be efficient and focused, not distracted by any drama or emotional feelings they may have. It's easy for me to frame a problem and clearly see the best course of action, so I can get frustrated with people who are wishy-washy. It's such a waste of time to keep hashing over options once we're reached a decision. I always work toward meeting a goal—in each case and in life, in general. For instance, I am on track to take my family to all the national parks within the next five years.

The Acting style. In the Acting style individuals take assertive, goal-directed action to get things done. They balance Experiencing and Thinking, while spending the least amount of time on Reflecting. They combine their ability to find solutions based on technical analysis with their attention to the needs of people and sources of information in concrete situations. They are equally comfortable in a practical world that can make use of their feelings and actions as well as in situations that that require their thinking abilities. As a result, they excel in identifying and integrating task and people needs.

Those who prefer the Acting style implement, execute, coordinate, and drive toward the finish line. They lead work teams, rally the troops, and speak up. They are on time, assertive, achievement-oriented, and fearless. If someone overuses the Acting style, he dreads the word *wait* and takes risks to be successful, even while sometimes aiming at the wrong target or clinging to one way of getting things done without reflecting about whether a different approach might be better.

Miguel, a manufacturing manager, prefers the Acting style. He says,

I definitely use Acting to approach life—at work and at home, I get right to the task at hand. I like to get things done. That means that I jump in and take some risks. When I have an order to produce, I mobilize all resources to get things moving. Time is money! If it's a new order and we have to reconfigure our line, I have my go-to people who will interpret the important information I need to make decisions. Whether on the manufacturing floor or in the office, I can switch gears quickly to get the order out on time. My team kids me that my favorite line during any team meeting is, 'OK, who's doing what by when?' as I tap my watch. As long as I surround myself with people who make sure that we are aiming at the right target, I am the go-to guy to get to things done.

The Initiating style. Those who use the Initiating style strive to complete projects and then seek new opportunities. They learn primarily through Acting and

Experiencing (feeling), paying the least attention to Analyzing. They enjoy achieving goals and involving themselves in new and challenging experiences. Their tendency may be to act on intuitive "gut" feelings rather than on logical analysis. In solving problems, individuals who prefer an Initiating style rely heavily on other people for information than on their own technical analysis.

Those who prefer the Initiating style think on their feet, back a hunch, network, and influence. They are outgoing, spontaneous, and able to shrug off losses or "failure" in favor of trying again. If someone overuses the initiating style, she dreads the words *status quo* and may be impulsive, pushy, and impatient.

Noor, a marketing executive, identifies with the Initiating style:

My ability to see opportunities and move to action immediately has served me well in marketing for our organizaiton. Our business environment changes so quickly that if we hesitate, we lose. Yes, sometimes we goof, but we recover quickly, and, just as often, we have big wins, so it's well worth taking some risks in the end. I often have to remind myself that other people just don't process things as quickly as I do, so I tap my persuasiveness to get them on board when I spot a good opportunity. I must admit that I can get impatient when others on my team are indecisive or want to spend too much time checking facts. After all, we can always tweak things once we get going, right?

The Balancing style. The Balancing style manages to stay away from the extremes of Acting, Reflecting, Experiencing, or Thinking by finding a middle ground between them. Taking this central position allows them to see many different perspectives on issues and bridge differences between people with different styles. They are often creative but may experience difficulty in making decisions.

Those who prefer the Balancing style weigh the pros and cons of the other learning styles to become a jack-of-all-trades. They are aware, adaptive, and resourceful; they tend to fill in the gaps and pursue a variety of situations. In a team they often adapt to fill in the missing style needed to get the task done. If someone overuses the Balancing style, he dreads the word *commit* and may risk becoming a chameleon that adapts dutifully to the situation at hand without forming an opinion of his own.

Charlotte, a mediator, describes her realization that she prefers the Balancing style:

I agree that I prefer a Balancing style since I have trouble coming down on one side or the other—I even had trouble answering the questions on the KLSI. That's actually a quality that makes me pretty good at what I do as a mediator. I can always see another side to an issue, and I probably found the one career that plays to my strengths. I like the variety of meeting new people and moving on to a new challenge every few days, and I am creative in coming up with new ideas or solutions to almost any problem. I'm not sure what I would do otherwise. Sometimes I think that I just have too many interests, so novelty is more important to me than mastery. I am adaptable to situations, so I learn quickly. One of my strong suits is teamwork: I can relate to people with different style preferences, so I bridge gaps between them. Because I can see everyone's perspective, it is sometimes hard for me to to commit to one of my own.

Learning Style and Life Path

Your learning style has influenced the path you have taken in your life. You have developed a learning style like a habit because it works for you in dealing with challenges of all kinds. Culture, personality, educational specialization, career choice, and the immediate demands of your life situation influence which learning style you develop. Early in life we begin to specialize in a particular learning style through a process of accentuation. We find a sweet spot in the learning cycle and continue to develop that approach. Because we like to play to our strengths, we like to choose situations where our style works and avoid situations that require a different style.

An active child, for example, may have trouble sitting still in a traditional classroom. Yet, she finds happiness outdoors where she can explore and take initiative. Finding success in these activities leads to the development of greater skills in these areas and a desire to pursue this path of living further. She practices Initiating until it is a habitual way of approaching any situation. Eventually, this child may build a career that allows her to take initiative, perhaps by becoming an entrepreneur who is a courageous risk-taker.

As Myles Horton said "We make the road by walking."[1] In other words, our learning style and life path are not preordained. They shape each other and are based on the choices we make. When our life situation changes, we can respond by developing other styles to expand our learning power.

The relationship between learning style and life path can be shown in the case of Ken. From a young age, Ken loved to work with numbers, preferred to work alone, and found math to be an elegant language. He was successful in high school advanced placement courses, scored off the charts in standardized college entrance exams, and was accepted at the college of his choice. Ken loaded his schedule with as many finance and accounting classes as he could, finally deciding on an accounting major. This meant that Ken did not take many humanities or social science courses, but they did not interest him anyway. Now Ken is a successful accountant who practices with a large prestigious firm. He is skilled in developing a strategy to make sure that his clients pay just the taxes that they owe. His ability to focus on complex data and then apply the most advantageous accounting framework has made Ken the most renowned specialist at his firm. Because of this ability, Ken was not surprised to learn that his learning style was Analyzing. The style describes his preferences well: structured, methodical, and precise. He would rather be working with his computer than dealing with people, and he is likely to avoid situations that call for teamwork, mentoring associates, or having difficult conversations. Ken has developed his approach and specialized role in the accounting firm over time by finding an organized way of approaching most situations. For instance, Ken chose situations that allowed him to concentrate on numbers for long periods of time rather than unpredictable situations that required him to improvise without careful planning. So Ken's learning style strengths supported his career choice, and this career choice reinforced his learning style strengths through consistent practice.

Styles Run Deep in Our Approach to Life

Learning styles can become deeply engrained habits that are evident not just in how we think but also in our whole being: our emotions, perceptions, behaviors, and even in physical movements. We develop an approach and skills that are attuned to the life that we have chosen. Our learning style becomes our way of processing possibilities; when possible, we pursue situations that will allow us to be successful while others never "dawn" on us as options. Because they are holistic, learning styles guide us in all arenas of learning and life: the way we manage our careers and relationships, our beliefs and mindset, and the way we spend our leisure time.

Charlotte's story reveals how a person's learning style influences her way of being in the world. Charlotte had a strong preference for the Initiating style. Although she had practiced as a psychologist, she quickly became bored with seeing individual patients and focusing on their problems, especially since change happened so slowly. She preferred to make use of her Initiating skill of adapting to changing conditions. She learned that she could apply this skill to the organizational arena, where she coached teams on group dynamics. The work suited her because it allowed her to actively participate in situations using an improvisational approach. She focused on the big picture, motivating and inspiring her teams to reach new goals. Charlotte never shied away from a straight-shooting approach of naming the "elephant in the room." Her clients loved her! She could keep things moving because she was so good "on her feet." In groups, she clicked with one or two others who were quick studies, and the more deliberate people seemed to admire her moxie. Once she started working with an organization, she could always discover a new opportunity through the many relationships she built. Although Charlotte never measured the actual impact of her work with teams, she collected many testimonials about her impact in the moment. She knew that she left people feeling good after providing a positive experience during her group programs, but she sometimes wondered about the lasting impact she was having.

While others seemed to be exhaused by her pace, Charlotte thrived on the hustle and bustle of business travel and meeting new clients in new settings. To keep her business running smoothly and because she got lost in details, Charlotte hired a subcontractor to do her administrative work. Her husband, Laith, managed their home while she traveled. His work in pharmaceutical research was a perfect fit for his Analyzing style. He could focus deeply on an issue for months at a time, investigating the details from every angle. He admired Charlotte for her easy-going sociability and leadership. He called her his "ready, fire, aim" partner. In reality, Charlotte's quick decision making and Laith's deliberate approach to decisions caused some temporary friction at times, but Charlotte brushed it off to avoid any lasting rift.

They noticed other differences, too. Charlotte loved praise, but, since Laith valued constructive criticism, that's what he dished out. When they played golf together, Charlotte found pleasure in simply being outdoors with him; the competition of the game was an added benefit. Laith, on the other hand, took his game seriously. He was methodical in his approach to every shot and took great care to critique the condition of the greens and the length of the rough. When another twosome would play up close to them, Charlotte's first instinct was to ask them to join them. She loved meeting new people and making fresh connections. This was painful for Laith. His approach would have been to speed up to avoid contact. He would rather endure playing quickly to avoid two things that he detested even more: meeting someone new or pressuring himself to perform well with strangers. They knew each other well enough to accept and cover for each others' challenges.

Like Charolotte, whose Initiating style showed up in her feelings, perceptions, thoughts, and behaviors, learning style preferences guide you at your most basic level. The following comments illustrate how a strong preference in one learning style can impact choices in all arenas of life and can leave people unaware of other options that correspond to unfamiliar learning styles.

Experiencing: "I always perfer face-to-face meetings instead of phone calls or emails. It never dawns on me that others may find this ineffecient, unnecessary, or even painful."

Imagining: "My first instinct is to help my clients reach their goals. I automatically scan for ways to support them to become successful. Can I introduce them to someone, share a tip, or do something extra? It never dawns on me to do the same for myself.

Reflecting: "When I prepare for a presentation, I procrastinate. I will spend 99 percent of my time mulling over the content, and I leave only 1 percent of the time to actually practice. It never dawns on me to start with a presentation that is not absolutely perfect and to improve it through practice."

Analyzing: "I only answer email when I have the answer ready for the client. It so important to me to get the details of the issue right that it never dawns on me to let the client know that I am in the process of getting the answer for her."

Thinking: "I see problems everywhere. I search for what is wrong and offer critical feedback, even to my spouse. It never dawns of me to notice what is right or to offer praise."

Deciding: "I have a goal for everything I do. It's almost a game with me to see how efficient I can be. Maybe that's why I hate teamwork. Working with other people slows me down. It never dawns on me that the end product may be better than the status quo or that I might help someone else learn through the experience."

Acting: "I keep a checklist so that I get everything done. I work at lightening speed to tie up loose ends; even then, I am often railroaded by millions of demands. I am sometimes so busy that it never dawns on me to pause to make sure I am actually effective and not just busy."

Initiating: "My ability to seize on opportunities works to my benefit most of the time. It sure did when I recognized that I was not happy in my job. I immediately jumped ship to another company. It never dawned on me to do nothing or to wait to see what would happen next."

Balancing: "I can always react to what is what is needed or missing to keep things going smoothly. I scan for it all the time. But it never dawns on me to take the lead in making a decision or steering the course."

A specialized learning style can support you to be successful in one path. It also limits what you see as possible for others. The learning styles model and the influence of others with different style preferences than your own can be helpful in opening your eyes to transformative opportunities.

Using Your Learning Style Awareness

Understanding your unique learning preferences and capabilities provides a new lens of self-awareness. It allows you to match your style preference to the demands of any situation to increase learning effectiveness. Your learning style can also provide clues to why your performance might not be as strong as it could be in certain situations and suggest strategies for improvement. Learning style preferences help explain why some topics and tasks are interesting and others painful. Learning styles can also help explain why some people develop a fixed view of their ability to learn. Many people who did not do well in school develop the belief that they are stupid, but becoming aware of their learning style helps them realize that they simply learn in a different way than schools teach. Early research shows that teachers tend to teach the way they learn, and many teachers were drawn to teaching because of their abstract learning styles (Analyzing, Thinking, or Deciding). Students whose learning styles do not match the styles of their teachers may find themselves swimming upstream.

Learning Styles to Help Understand Others

The learning styles help to explain why we click with some people and not with others. For instance, Ethan prefers to work with colleagues who pay attention to the factual details that his Thinking style craves rather than those colleagues who "shoot from the hip" without regard for numbers and facts. Fatima, who prefers an Experiencing style, finds it impossible to connect with people who do not make eye contact when they speak. Christopher's Acting style allows him to kick into action as soon as a decision is made rather search for problems in the plan.

Learning styles can also help us interpret differences in the way people communicate. Individuals who prefer the Experiencing style speak about feelings and share stories while those who prefer the Thinking style will stick to the facts and hard data, keeping their emotions out of the equation. Likewise, the orientation of the message is different, even opposite, in various styles. For instance, those who prefer the Deciding style target their messages for practical results while those who prefer the Imagining style slow things down as they brainstorm new ideas. No wonder colleagues with those styles often feel at odds.

Timing and tone differ, too. People with a preference for the Acting style are quick to respond, usually in a commanding voice. When Maria, who prefers the Reflecting style, received the following email from Sarah, an Acting learner, she could feel herself closing down:

Subject: Tomorrow's Meeting

Message: Meet in the conference room at 12 to discuss new client approach! Budget attached.

How could Maria possibly offer her opinion when it seemed like the decisions regarding the new client had already been made? The exclamation mark alone left her feeling anxious. Maria prefers to take her time approaching tasks, while Sarah drives to achieve her goals in record time. Once Sarah and Maria were able to appreciate that their communication was related to their learning style preferences, they were more likely to read between the lines. They even tried to launch conversations in a way that promoted connection instead of friction.

Feedback preferences differ by learning style, too. People who prefer concrete experience—Initiating, Experiencing, and Imagining—thrive with appreciation of their positive accomplishments and what's going well, whereas those with abstract styles—Analyzing, Thinking, and Deciding—request critical evaluation for what is lacking and could be improved. Both approaches are needed over time, and neither is complete on its own.

Understanding other learning styles can help you approach people whose communication style differs from your own. You can bridge communication gaps by anticipating how people with different learning styles prefer to communicate. Table 3.2 provides general communication patterns for each learning style. It also includes addressing a conflict with someone who prefers that style and suggests the approach to take when things get tense.

68

Learning Style and Communication Patterns	Communication Tips
Experiencing	
General tendencies: Focuses on emotions and feelings, includes language that is sensitive and accepting (touched by a feeling, grounded, present, mindful, qualitative findings), and often uses stories and metaphors to convey information. In conversation, Experiencing communicators prefer to remain open, listen, accept, help, include, and empathize.	**Key Phrases:** "Something feels off to me." "How is everyone feeling?" **When addressing conflict:** Make it personal and warm. **When things get tense:** Acknowledge emotions and desire to feel good when you get through the bump in the road.
Imagining	
General tendencies: Uses words that convey empathy and trust (value ideas, brainstorm, reach for the stars, create an ideal vision, be understanding). In conversation, Imagining learners inquire by asking powerful questions that encourage instead of confront; they listen to understand and include everyone, drawing others out in conversation, taking a pulse on feelings.	**Key Phrases:** "How can I help?" "Let's imagine the possibilities." "What other information do we need?" **When addressing conflict:** Make a personal connection using values. **When things get tense:** Show warm, easy-going approach. Acknowledge emotions and intent to stay connected. Empathize and appeal to values.

Learning Style and Communication Patterns	Communication Tips
Reflecting	
General tendencies: Communicates slowly and thoughtfully (take time, be cautious, pause, process the idea, watch a role model). Reflecting communicators ask powerful questions to go deeper, listen carefully, and weigh words and ideas carefully prior to speaking.	**Key Phrases:** "Let me explore this further." "Can I get back to you after I have time to think this through?" or simply be silent. **When addressing conflict:** Go slowly and ask questions. **When things get tense:** Use patience; take it easy. Allow for time alone before making decisions.
Analyzing	
General tendencies: Uses concise, logical language (seek details, organize the facts, synthesize the data, use research, create a plan). Analyzing communicators attend to details, use theories to test assumptions, and provide conceptual models to process ideas before applying them.	**Key Phrases:** "Let's focus on the details." "What theories or models explain?" "Are my thoughts organized? **When addressing conflict:** Focus on facts; value their expertise and contribution. **When things get tense:** Acknowledge their command of content, use theories or models to guide. Respect uniqueness. Do not become emotional.
Thinking	
General tendencies: Communicates logically and rationally (see the point, just the facts, focus on issues, make a thorough spreadsheet, use quantitative information, one objective, cost/benefit.) Thinking communicators focus on a logical progression of facts and are able to back up claims with numbers.	**Key Phrases:** "Where are the numbers that prove this point?" "I see a problem here." "What evidence do you have?" **When addressing conflict:** Get to the point by focusing on facts and figures. Expect skepticism. **When things get tense:** Step back and be objective. Downplay emotions. Remain logical.

Learning Style and Communication Patterns	Communication Tips
Deciding	
General tendencies: Uses language that is clear, pragmatic, direct, and efficient (take a practical approach, measure success, critical feedback, strong direction, best practice). Deciding communicators focus on practical results, measuring success and committing to one goal.	**Key Phrases:** "Here's our goal." "How will we know if we succeed?" "Take this direction." **When addressing conflict:** Make efficient use of time. Be clear, direct, and purposeful. Expect skepticism. **When things get tense:** Set clear, practical goals and use technical problem solving, clear standards of success. Provide comparisons. Focus on how to reach a mutual goal.
Acting	
General tendencies: Communicates dynamically and rapidly, in a commanding tone (take action, quick turnaround, achieve results, implement the plan). Acting communicators focus on checklists and the urgency to complete them; they return phone calls immediately and focus on getting things accomplished.	**Key Phrases:** "Let's do this!" "Who does what by when?" "What is the one action we can take now?" "Time is money." **When addressing conflict:** Be purposeful and direct. Show concern for people and issues. Focus on getting things done quickly. **When things get tense:** Take a walk together. Do something that moves toward resolution. Allow discharge of feelings and do not take it personally.

Learning Style and Communication Patterns	Communication Tips
Initiating	
General tendencies: Communicates with persuasiveness, improvises to adjust, and uses inspiring, energetic language (set the pace, grab the prize, seize the opportunity). Makes connections and influences to seize opportunities.	**Key Phrases:** "Let's go with it." "Don't miss out." "You can do this." **When addressing conflict:** Show optimism and enthusiasm. Use humor that is nonjudgmental. **When things get tense:** Remain open to change. Expect spontaneity and rapid-fire questions. Face situations quickly and directly.
Balancing	
General: Remains flexible when communicating. (Balances the situation, includes variety, is adaptive, takes holistic perspective). Balancing communicators show verbal and nonverbal flexibility.	**Key Phrases:** "On one hand … yet, on the other hand …" "We have a blind spot." **When addressing conflict:** Be appreciative and cheerful so they will respond in kind. Be adaptable. **When things get tense:** Allow them to identify options and blind spots. Collaborate and share solution.

Table 3.2 Communication Preferences by Learning Style

Connecting the Nine Learning Styles to the Learning Cycle

The nine learning styles connect to nine steps in any process or project—problem solving, decision-making, and even teamwork. By expanding the four-step learning cycle process to the new nine-step full cycle, you will have more detail to walk you through any situation successfully. Since the learning cycle process is holistic, each step in the process relates to a portion of you as a fully developed person. Review Figure 3.2 to see which steps in this expanded learning cycle process you use and which you avoid. The figure adds the styles of Imagining, Analyzing, Deciding, Initiating, and Balancing to the four-step learning cycle of Experiencing, Reflecting, Thinking, and Acting.

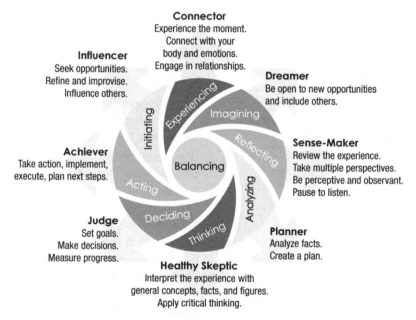

Figure 3.2 Learning Styles as Steps in the Learning Cycle Process

Using Learning Styles with High Performance Teams

When individuals have an awareness of each other's learning styles, they can work together on high performance teams that achieve exceptional results.

Members' preferred styles correspond to a step in the learning cycle process.

Lisa and her team of nurses quickly understood the value of using the concepts of the learning cycle and learning styles. Already aware of her affinity for getting things accomplished, Lisa recognized her preference for the Deciding style, yet she could identify times when she used other ways of learning, too. Lisa found it easier to work with people who shared a preference for the Deciding style, but she realized that teamwork was more successful when she worked with people who had different style preferences from her own. When a diverse team was able to use the strengths of all of their styles as they spiraled around the learning cycle to complete their work, Lisa felt a synergy that she did not feel when she worked with colleagues whose styles were similar to her own.

The learning styles model helped Lisa to see the natural tensions on her team: James valued process, a hallmark of his Reflecting style; Ava and Pierre's Initiating style preference showed up when they pushed for quick outcomes and getting the work accomplished on time. Rachel preferred the Imagining style, which put her directly opposite Lisa's preference on the learning cycle. While Rachel preferred to generate lots of ideas and gather more information, Lisa wanted to focus on one option. This can put them at odds. Lisa could recognize her own preference for task over relationship. As she reflected on her previous experiences with teams, she realized that she found them to be inefficient and exhausting. When she could judge so early and commit to action, what took others so long?

As she looked at the learning styles model, Lisa recognized that she often skipped over the Experiencing, Imagining, and Reflecting ways of learning. Also, she could draw parallels about the ways in which her profession had changed over the past two decades. She wondered whether a focus on data-driven electronic medical records encouraged nurses to underfocus on relationships and patient experience, empathy, and taking time with patients, in general. Lisa hoped that an intentional focus on learning styles would allow her team to be more innovative and effective.

Lisa's entire team identified their learning style preferences and mapped them out around the learning cycle. This allowed everyone to see which parts of the learning cycle the other team members preferred and which they avoided, as you can see in Figure 3.3.

The team's learning strengths and challenges became clear, and the steps of the learning cycle that did not correspond to anyone's learning style required careful attention. For instance, Lisa noticed that no one on the team had a preference for Experiencing, Analyzing, Thinking, or Acting styles. She would need to pay special attention to these steps in the team process since no other member would necessarily focus on them. Lisa was hoping that some of her colleagues would have strengths in areas that she had not yet developed so that she could share leadership at critical junctures. For instance, Rachel's Imagining style preference would allow her to take the lead to generate new ideas before the team committed to one course of action. Lisa's Deciding style would ensure that the team did not linger in the Imagining step for too long. Pierre's Initiating style could also move the team to action when they got stuck.

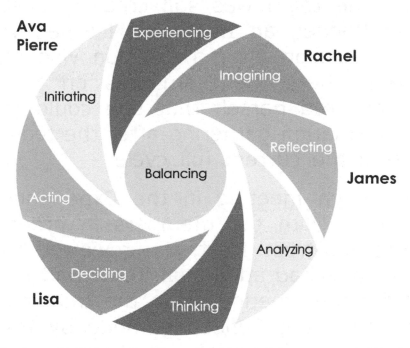

Figure 3.3 Lisa's Team Map of Learning Styles

Lisa used the learning cycle as a process guide for every meeting: Experiencing, Imagining, Reflecting, Analyzing, Thinking, Deciding, Acting, and Initiating were steps associated with tasks and behaviors. At any moment in the work of the team she could identify where they were on the learning cycle. This allowed the team to stay on task and know what to do next. It also helped to keep them on the same page as they worked together. Lisa found that when she referred to the learning cycle, team members were able to get back on track and did not take things personally. They also seemed to enjoy paying attention to how their styles served them well or not. For instance, Ava, who preferred the Initiating style, could notice when she was impatient to get things started even when the team was still creating a solid plan. Also, when Rachel, an Imagining learner, wanted to reopen a discussion after a decision was made, she remembered where the team was on the learning cycle and assured herself that she could revisit the need for information gathering after the team finished implementing the current full cycle.

Lisa began each meeting in the Experiencing mode by checking in with the members in order to build relationships and trust. Next, Lisa reviewed the agenda to see if anyone had additional items and to set ideal outcomes for the meeting using the Imagining mode. She encouraged the Reflecting mode by taking time for discussion and asking incisive questions that allowed them to take many perspectives and to minimize mistakes. Next, the team used the Analyzing mode by organizing the information so they could begin to make a plan. Lisa included time for the Thinking mode in the meeting agenda so the members could critically evaluate all the options before making a decision. Once the team used the Deciding mode to commit to a focused goal, Lisa switched to the Acting mode. She always said, "OK, who does what by when?" They would set a date for their next meeting and leave with clear accountability for implementation.

Lisa encouraged team members to pay attention to their learning style, use the learning cycle intentionally as they completed their individual work between meetings, and share key learning points with colleagues. When team members acknowledged having difficulty with a step in the process, other members felt empowered to offer assistance.

Learning styles provide a foundation for team members to understand their preferences when working individually and together. As members create a map of their learning style preferences, teams can see which of the portions of the learning cycle they have covered and which portions they might be prone to skip. As head of a team of intensive care unit nurses, Pierre, true to his Initiating style, could not wait to introduce the learning styles model to all the unit's nursing staff. After mapping their learning style preferences, the staff realized that they largely favored Deciding, Acting, and Initiating styles. By exploring their learning styles and the learning cycle, the staff members recognized that their styles supported their quickly moving to action to achieve exceptional results in urgent situations. However, they also acknowledged that when they were on automatic pilot, they could overlook how they related to patients, their families, and each other; ignore others' opinions; or discount the importance of the processes they used.

Pierre's own style preference of Initiating supported him as a leader who could institute a team learning approach, yet he recognized that he often skipped over other steps in the learning cycle. To include these missing steps in the team process Pierre planned time for the Experiencing mode to build relationships and trust. He used the Imagining mode by making sure to include the opinions of all team members and allowing time to consider new possibilities rather than deciding on outcomes too early. To encourage the Reflecting mode, Pierre and the team took time to discuss their process and check their assumptions at regular intervals. During one of these meetings, David, who was a notable exception with his Analyzing preference, felt comfortable enough to share his idea for a new approach to a quality control issue. This information was pivotal to the team's success in solving the problem and inspiring innovation for the entire unit. David then led the team during the Reflecting and Analyzing steps: he made sense of the information from many perspectives, synthesized information, and created a plan. In addition, David experienced an entirely new level of engagement and loyalty after having a direct impact on the team's outcome. He even led the group's effort to publish their findings.

As Lisa and Pierre discovered, learning styles offer insight regarding who might share leadership at various steps of the learning process. For instance, a Reflecting learner may guide the team during the problem analysis phase while an Acting learner can step into a leadership role during the implementation phase. Table 3.3 illustrates the typical strengths of each learning style when working within a team.

Initiating	Experiencing	Imagining
<ul><li>Seizing opportunities</li><li>Initiating action</li><li>Providing optimism and influence</li></ul>	<ul><li>Being aware of the situation</li><li>Focusing on relationships</li><li>Providing connection and environmental support</li></ul>	<ul><li>Generating ideas</li><li>Including others and their opinions</li><li>Providing inspiration and inclusion</li></ul>
Acting	**Balancing**	**Reflecting**
<ul><li>Implementing a plan</li><li>Executing for completion</li><li>Keeping time and driving for results</li></ul>	<ul><li>Monitoring for blind spots</li><li>Focusing on adapting</li><li>Bridging the gaps when perspectives differ</li></ul>	<ul><li>Analyzing problems</li><li>Reviewing options</li><li>Providing patience and perspective</li></ul>
Deciding	**Thinking**	**Analyzing**
<ul><li>Making practical decisions</li><li>Converging around a goal and measuring progress</li><li>Providing practicality and commitment</li></ul>	<ul><li>Analyzing solutions</li><li>Reaching conclusions</li><li>Providing skepticism and logic</li></ul>	<ul><li>Synthesizing information</li><li>Planning to minimize mistakes</li><li>Providing organized data and structuring an approach</li></ul>

Table 3.3 Learning Styles to Guide Shared Leadership on Teams

Applying Your Knowledge of Learning Styles

As you learn how understand yourself as a learner, you can be aware of how your style preference impacts your own success. You can become so deeply attached to doing what you do best that you unconsciously screen out possibilities to practice different styles, limiting the opportunities for growth that exist outside your comfort zone.

The awareness of the parts of the learning cycle that you favor and those that you don't can lay a framework for your development. As a coach Madeleine used her awareness of learning style to increase her effectiveness with clients. Her preference for the Experiencing style and backup styles in Imagining and Reflecting allowed her to connect with her client, establish trust, show empathy, identify an ideal outcome, and inquire patiently during their session. However, her attachment to feelings and intuition sometimes left her short in planning, identifying patterns, and locking in to a goal for long-term achievement and change. To manage these potential downsides, Madeleine was careful to attend to goal setting early in the session and to pay attention to the time so that the client would leave with clear measures of accountability.

Madeleine's coaching colleague, Ron, found that his Deciding style kept him on time and task, but sometimes he judged too early. He managed his tendency to drive to practical outcomes by carving out ten minutes of every session to explore possible outcomes and to inquire carefully. Interestingly, his reputation for being a strict performance-oriented coach seemed to attract different clients from Madeleine. She seemed to work with more clients who were managing difficult relationships or seeking work-life balance.

If you have never thought about your approach to learning, you are not alone. Learning seems so automatic that few people consider what the learning process is or how they approach it. As you recognize your learning style and your distinctive strengths and challenges, you will also recognize the ways of learning that are not yet in your comfort zone.

Entrenchment occurs when you habitually cling to your preferred learning style. Studies have shown that when people specialize in one field, especially highly technical or abstract fields like science, medicine, law, or engineering, they tend to be more rigidly attached to one learning style. This may make them more successful in their specialty, but it leaves them with less flexibility to use other learning styles. What makes the specialist successful in his or her chosen career may contribute to less overall flexibility in life. Building learning flexibility, the next step in the learning way, is the antidote.

Learning Style Checklist for Action

Use the following checklist to remind you how to build self-awareness through understanding your learning style.

- Identify your learning style preference by taking the KLSI 4.0 (see Appendix A).

- Monitor the way you navigate the learning cycle, paying attention to the learning ways that you use and the ones that are unfamiliar.

- On a team, map the learning style preferences of your team members. Use the steps in the learning cycle to guide a team activity or decision, and describe the team process and outcome in terms of the nine steps of the full learning cycle process.

- Identify the learning styles of your coworkers, friends, and family members and compare their strengths to the skills that you need to succeed.

Practice

Several times throughout the day, pay attention to the situation and notice how your learning style is guiding you. When trying to solve a problem or make a decision, notice which step of the process is required and how you adapt to address each step.

Reflection

You may find it helpful to journal about your preferred learning style. Below you will find prompts for your reflections:

- What are the strengths and challenges of your learning style?

- How has your learning style supported you in your life path?

- Describe a typical "day in your life." Identify your typical learning approach by highlighting the part of the learning cycle process that you seek out as you note the activities you prefer and the ones you avoid. Include information about how you approach

  * Time and obligations

  * People and relationships

  * Work, home, and family

  * Emotions

  * Communication and feedback

- Create a personal portfolio that represents your preferred learning style. This can include poetry, personal photos, journal entries, writings about interactions and relationships, favorite activities, and lists of strengths and personal challenges. Notice the many ways in which your style impacts your feelings, perceptions, thoughts, and actions.

- Compose an email. Now try to assume different learning styles and alter the message to reflect the orientation of each of the styles.

- Make a list of the strengths of your personal style. Consider how you use these every day at work and play. Then make a list of the strengths of the style opposite to yours. Write a brief statement on how the acknowledgment of this interdependent opposite can be useful and supportive.

- Think of a character in a novel or a movie that has always resonated with you. Determine the learning style of the character. How does this compare to your learning style? Is it similar to your own or completely opposite?

Chapter Four

Building Style Flexibility

Things do not change; we change.

Henry David Thoreau

Your learning style helps you to be successful because you gravitate to situations that call for the skills associated with your style. Through repeated practice, you become more capable of dealing with situations that demand the capabilities of your preferred style. People seek stability, so they typically match their life situation with their preference in order to stay within their comfort zone. But what happens when your need for stability makes you feel brittle and uncertain? Or what if you avoid situations that can make you more successful or effective? You can increase your comfort zone by building learning flexibility.

Learning flexibility is the ability to use all the learning styles in response to various situations. You can use the information in this chapter to expand your learning style repertoire to include the styles you do not currently use. You will explore the many benefits of building learning flexibility for your own effectiveness in learning and life. Finally, you will have the opportunity to choose one learning style goal that will help you to become more flexible.

The following story about Anne Robinson illustrates how learning flexibility helped her to respond to challenges that she encountered and build a highly successful career.

Although petite, Anne's striking presence and seriousness make her appear immovable and unshakable. She draws you in as she keeps her distance. She simultaneous screams "you want my approval" and "approach with caution." Anne carefully cultivated this strong persona in the late 1990s when she became the "Queen of Mean" on a successful BBC and NBC television show *The Weakest Link.* The long-running series provided a platform for her quick, caustic wit as she infamously intimidated and rattled contestants.

Anne's toughness was fostered by her mother who had been an unusual role model of how to succeed in a man's world with no excuses. Her mother built a small market into the largest food chain in northern England. Every night at the dinner table, Anne and her mother would discuss how much money they had made, which customers they should keep, and which they should ditch. By taking some carefully managed risks, they built confidence unknown by many women of the day. Their goal orientation and commitment to success became a central part of their approach to life. Playing to her strengths, Anne further developed her ability to make a case and take a stand when she became a journalist, working for every major paper in Britain before joining the BBC as a broadcaster.

Eventually, Anne's focus on toughness made her brittle and broken. The bravery that had allowed her to take risks turned into reckless, destructive behavior. At her lowest moments in her mid-thirties, she was a nonfunctioning alcoholic who had deteriorated to seventy-five pounds, too ill to keep custody of her only daughter. Eventually, Anne decided to use her natural toughness to work on herself, picked herself up, and used her journalistic talents to write a book about the dreadful experience, entered TV, and became one of the most recognized journalists in Britain. Following *The Weakest Link,* Anne hosted a prime-time consumer watchdog show for fifteen years and transitioned to making documentaries and championing a charitable cause.

During that transition, Anne decided that her strengths—decisiveness and toughness—were no longer serving her well. She sought to develop partnerships and engage others to join in her charitable cause, skills that require building lasting relationships. She had to moderate her "Queen of Mean" attitude by developing more soft edges and empathy. She learned to soften her smirk into a smile, balancing both grit and grace to make each quality exponentially more effective. Anne developed the ability to be flexible in her approach to learning through life's challenges, helping her understand who she is now and who she wants to become.

Anne's initial strong preference for the Deciding style provided a foundation for her success early in life. She was able to form strong arguments to make her case and then deliver it with decisive commitment. This stable and specialized approach focused on her strengths but left her with little access to the styles associated with other ways of learning. As Anne's life progressed and her responsibilities increased, she needed to develop more range. She developed additional backup capabilities in Acting and Initiating, Thinking and Analyzing—the styles adjacent to the Deciding style on the learning cycle. These capabilities allowed her to plan strategically and take charge while driving her and others to extraordinary achievements. In her work for a charitable cause, Anne began meeting with donors to enlist their personal and financial support using the Thinking style to focus on how the charity adds value to society and on the Deciding style to set goals for getting their donations. Her direct, assertive approach was not working, so Anne needed to consider a different approach. She believed that she would be more successful if she connected with donors through her strong positive emotions about the charity by harnessing the Experiencing style. The Experiencing style would be a better match when she needed to form relationships that didn't rely on her commands but on connections. The Imagining style could also help her seek the opinions of many stakeholders before she made decisions, and the Reflecting style could allow Anne to slow down and allow space for others to offer their perspectives in those situations. By adding these learning styles to her repertoire, Anne saw that instead of barking witty yet potentially biting off-the-cuff remarks, she could have more positive interactions with empathy, listening, and observing.

Learning Flexibility

You can use the nine styles of learning described in chapter three to transform your life. These nine ways of learning provide you with a complete set of skills to creatively manage any situation and learn in the process. Developing the capability to use them all enables you to tap the full power of the learning cycle, and your own full potential. Table 4.1 describes the nine ways of learning and their associated capabilities.

Initiating	Experiencing	Imagining
■ Flexibly adapting to changing context and conditions ■ Influencing and motivating others ■ Recognizing new opportunities ■ Bouncing back from failure	■ Establishing trusting relationships ■ Being involved and engaged ■ Connecting personally when communicating ■ Being comfortable with emotional expression	■ Generating new ideas ■ Demonstrating empathy for others ■ Seeking others' opinions ■ Imagining new possibilities
Acting	**Balancing**	**Reflecting**
■ Meeting time deadlines ■ Finding ways to make things happen ■ Taking goal-oriented action to achieve results ■ Implementing plans with limited resources	■ Identifying the blind spots in a whole situation ■ Bridging differences between people ■ Adapting to shifting priorities ■ Displaying resourcefulness	■ Listening with an open mind ■ Gathering information from a variety of sources ■ Identifying underlying problems and issues ■ Viewing issues from many perspectives
Deciding	**Thinking**	**Analyzing**
■ Finding practical solutions to problems ■ Committing to a goal ■ Making decisions and solving problems ■ Taking a stand, even on controversial issues	■ Using quantitative evidence to analyze solutions ■ Framing arguments with logic ■ Using critical thinking for objective communication ■ Making independent judgments	■ Planning ahead to minimize mistakes ■ Organizing information to get the full picture ■ Analyzing data ■ Using theories and models to explain issues

Table 4.1 The Nine Styles of Learning and their Associated Capabilities

Learning flexibility, the ability to develop capabilities in all styles of learning, allows you to creatively match your approach to the situation at hand. If you are meeting someone new, you may benefit from using the Experiencing or Imagining style rather than the Analyzing or Thinking style; however, if you are conducting a cost-to-benefit analysis, Experiencing and Imagining are probably not the best choice for this problem. You will probably do better by using the Thinking and Deciding styles. Learning flexibility and mobility within the learning cycle are antidotes for the rigidity of a specialized learning style. The more flexibility you develop, the more freedom and confidence you'll have in meeting situations as they arise. Learning flexibility also sets you up to move toward an integrated life.

By taking the KLSI 4.0, you will receive a measurement of your learning flexibility. The Learning Flexibility Index of the KLSI 4.0 measures your ability to capitalize on the strengths of other learning styles. This score quantifies how much you "flex" to other styles and identifies which learning styles you use as a backup. See Appendix A for more information about the KLSI 4.0.

Like Anne, most of us have a dominant learning style and an array of backup styles that we use to more effectively meet the demands of various learning situations. This is important when our own preference is not the best match. If you have a strongly defined learning style, you have well-developed skills associated with that part of the learning cycle. At the same time your skills in some other styles and parts of the learning cycle may not be so strong. This often occurs with opposing style pairs on the learning cycle, the style that is directly opposite from your preferred dominant style. For example, an individual who is at home in the Thinking style may feel like a fish out of water in the nonlogical world of concrete feelings in the Experiencing style. When a situation arises that demands skills outside his home region, he faces a dilemma in approaching the situation with his comfortable learning style or trying another learning style. Over time, his most effective approach is to build strength in backup styles—to flex to meet the situation more effectively.

Consider Harry, who has a learning style preference of Analyzing. When Harry is completing his tax returns, he is well matched to the learning task that requires organizing and calculating financial data, being focused on details. However, when Harry plays golf, his Analyzing style preference may not be the best match for an enjoyable game. Playing golf may be better matched to those styles that link doing and feeling, such as the Acting and Experiencing styles. Certainly, Harry will benefit from using the entire learning cycle during his round—paying attention to his movement as he hits the ball, reflecting on his swing and the outcome, analyzing to make a plan, drawing on general knowledge, setting a goal for the next shot, and then repeating the process. However, Harry can be most effective if he leads with a learning style that best matches this situation. The switch from accounting to golf affected which part of the learning cycle was most critical to the situation and determined which style would allow Harry to meet it most effectively. Because his preferred style was not an ideal match for the situation, he can benefit by flexing to a backup style that more closely fits the context.

Building Flexibility to Match Situations

Awareness of the importance of learning flexibility alone may be enough to build flexibility in nondominant styles. Kyle, the chief financial officer of a rapidly growing tech company, had a strong attachment to the Analyzing style, an approach that supported his specialization in the high stakes of finance. Kyle was a one-man department performing numerous functions at a critical juncture for the organization. He rarely had a free moment and often took work home with him, especially on Wednesday afternoons when he left work early to take over the childcare of his two-year old daughter Sophia. Kyle tried to time his arrival just after his wife has put Sophia down for her nap so that he could work for an hour or two without the interruptions he experienced at the office. However, whenever Sophia did not fall asleep on schedule, Kyle felt his mood shift to frustration; this not only impacted his ability to enjoy being with his daughter, it also carried over into blaming his wife for arriving home late.

After being introduced to the learning way, Kyle quickly identified his own preference for the Analyzing style. He saw that all the steps in the learning cycle were necessary to the financial decision-making process and how his most successful outcomes included every step in the process. Kyle recognized that his preferred Analyzing style was the best choice in his work as a CFO, yet it left him and his family short when he used it to approach some situations at home.

Armed with this information, Kyle decided to improve his time with Sophia by embracing a different learning style. The following Wednesday, he left his briefcase at the office and went home with a plan to "show up and be present" for whatever Sophia needed rather than arriving with a rigid plan for how he would spend his time. He entered the situation using the Experiencing style by being present in the moment, connecting with his daughter in a way that he had not been able to do when he was distracted by work. He played with her, rested with her, and did chores around the house with her at his side. He even gave her little tasks in the kitchen so that she could "help" him make dinner. When Kyle's wife came home braced for the usual barrage of complaints, she was mystified and amazed to find a happy child and a relaxed husband. Not only did Kyle find a new way to relate to his family, he discovered that he was more effective when he returned to work later in the evening to briefly tie up loose ends.

As Kyle continued to practice using the Experiencing style at work, he realized how deeply engrained his Analyzing style was. His first inclination was to see problems and seek data everywhere, even in relationships with colleagues. As he focused on appreciating his relationships with others, he began to catch himself if he became critical or rigidly attached to a plan when it was unnecessary and not the best style match.

Kyle's specialized Analyzing learning style helped him to become successful in his career by giving him a firm foundation for work that was a good fit: he enjoyed the world of finance and was exceptional at mastering strategy and tactics. However, Kyle's specialized learning style had limitations, too. He found that his Analyzing approach was not such a good match for building relationships at home or at the office. As Kyle's company grows, he may expand his department and begin managing teams. His preferred Analyzing style is not the best approach for setting departmental goals or coaching individual contributors to reach those goals, making learning flexibility even more important for Kyle's continued success. By building flexibility in the Experiencing style, Kyle is setting himself up to build flexibility in other styles, too.

Another flexibility-building strategy is to stop overusing your own preferred style. Catherine did just that. She dampened the effects of her strong preference for the Acting style to flexibly connect with a client who had a different learning style. The Acting style had allowed Catherine to make it in a man's world when she became one of the first female litigation partners in a prestigious midsized law firm. The approach continued to serve her well as she developed new business while maintaining her exemplary win-loss record in the courtroom.

When Catherine first became aware of the learning styles, she exclaimed, "Now my client makes sense to me, and I understand why she is frustrated with me, too!" Catherine described a client interaction that involved a person with a preference for the Reflecting style. Catherine had been trying to get the person to file a time-sensitive lawsuit; the more Catherine pushed, the more the client hesitated. Catherine said, "I have been trying to do what I do best, only harder. The more I try to move her to action, the more she entrenches in reflection. We are both retreating to our home styles from the urgent pressure just at the moment when we should be more flexible." The next time Catherine called her client, she held back from interrupting or telling the client what to do. She later reported that by slowing down her process and even changing the pace with which she spoke, she was able to listen carefully to her client's concerns. This shift allowed her to build rapport with her client in a way that had previously been impossible. Catherine also admitted to learning some new information about the case that the client had been too embarrassed to reveal, information that ultimately proved invaluable in the courtroom.

Catherine applied her understanding of learning styles to situations at home, too. She recognized that her husband had a style preference that complemented her own. Even though it made them two halves of a perfect whole as they approached the learning cycle, it also meant that she was frustrated by his cautious orientation toward risk taking. In order to connect with him more deeply, she stopped herself from relying on the Acting style to employ what she had learned about leading with the Reflecting style. Whenever she initiated a difficult conversation, instead of launching into the discussion with a declarative statement, she began with a carefully crafted question that sought his perspective and feelings.

Recognizing what each situation calls for increases your learning effectiveness. While you will be most successful if you build all the capabilities of the learning cycle, you will benefit from leading with different styles in various contexts. In some situations an emphasis on Experiencing may produce the best results, while others may require logical analysis. For instance, decision making in general is an evaluative, thinking activity focused on choosing the best outcome or course of action. Yet, a decision about what restaurant to go to might demand a focus on the Experiencing style while a decision about which stocks to buy could benefit from the Analyzing style. Similarly, planning in general may rely on the

Reflecting, Analyzing, and Thinking styles when you organize a systematic plan of action; however, the specific plan you need to make might influence your approach—planning a party may require the Experiencing style while planning a budget would call for the Thinking or Analyzing styles.

A typical approach to building flexibility involves deeply exploring your own style and gradually trying out a nondominant style. As you become aware of using your learning style, you can begin to expand step by step, using the learning cycle as your guide. For example, Juan, who is strongly attached to the Reflecting style, carefully planned his learning experiments to improve his ability to use the Acting style, especially when he was meeting in groups. Rather than observing, he wanted to participate by offering an opinion. He used his powers of observation to watch role models, and then he practiced in his head before acting. While practicing, he noticed his experience and then reflected on what went well and what he could do better. From there, he set a new strategy and tried again, creating a new experience and a new spiral of the learning cycle. He was patient in his approach, but he needed to push himself to try new behaviors as he built his capabilities in the Acting style. For instance, Juan found he was more at ease if he offered an opinion early in the meeting rather than waiting until the last minute when he pressured himself to perform. Regardless of when, he knew that the practice of using the Acting style was critical to his learning.

This is a different approach from Susan, who preferred the Deciding style. Susan was able to commit to building her Imagining style capabilities such as being empathetic and generating novel ideas. Because Susan leans more toward the Thinking and Acting styles, she objectively measured her results against a standard and then tried again. For instance, Susan noticed if she was able to feel empathy for every person on her team as she was building her new skill. If she did not connect with someone, she engaged in a conversation to get to know her or him better. She needed to remind herself to connect with her own experience and to remain open to new ideas as she drives herself toward self-improvement.

Your learning mindset will be important as you begin to experiment with new learning styles. You will be temporarily out of your comfort zone. Seek ways to intentionally practice your desired style by planning ahead, and pay attention to what works and what you need to revise.

Building Flexibility from Experience

Regardless of which learning style you are trying to develop, remember that learning is a process, one that requires knowledge of the learning cycle and your own style. You start by focusing on your own experience. While you can read about concepts and theories, your individual experience in the world is unique. Therefore, begin with your own experience and use the strengths of your style to guide you through the full learning cycle. Be aware of when you need a backup style to more successfully meet the demands of a situation and try using it.

Learning flexibility—the ability to use all nine learning styles based on the situation at hand—helps individuals to be at the top of their game: the leader who approaches issues with both wisdom and courage; the physician who can connect emotionally with a patient while providing technically sophisticated care; the entrepreneur who can create a product and sell it, too. These individuals have a dominant learning style and backup styles that include many of the other learning styles, perhaps even those that are opposite from their preferred style. You are capable of acquiring this well-rounded, adaptable presence if you choose to develop all the learning styles. No expression of a style is right or wrong; you will find your own way of using each one. In the short term, you may choose to surround yourself with people who complement your preferred style in order to compensate for the skills you have not yet developed. Over the long term, you will be well served by developing the capabilities associated with all the learning styles.

Access to an expanded repertoire of learning styles allows you to expand your comfort zone. People who have high learning flexibility have greater overall flexibility in life. They see more possibilities in any given moment, they experience less conflict and stress, and they are able to handle more complexity. Flexible people also are more self-directed, so they are more likely to make changes that help them adapt to unexpected situations. Last but not least, they are happier!

When Is It Difficult to Develop Learning Flexibility?

If flexibility is so beneficial, why doesn't everyone develop it easily? The deeper we are attached to our preferred learning style, the more we may see the opposite style as foreign or negative. So, how can we get unstuck when inertia has us locked into our preferred learning style? We must recognize that we value the upside of our preferred learning style so much that we overtolerate its downside. We tolerate the downside of our preferred learning style because we fear the downsides of other styles. For instance, Ellie, a marketing manager, had a strong preference for the Imagining style. She thrived on keeping her choices open so that she would not miss opportunities. However, Ellie often had trouble reaching her goals. Ellie was so attached to her preferred style of Imagining and the skills of appreciating diversity, feeling empathy, and being open and receptive that she overused this style. Her focus on the Imagining style caused her to underutilize the Deciding style, the opposite style on the learning cycle. Her inability to make decisions impacted her effectiveness, but Ellie overtolerated the downside of the Imagining style because she is avoiding the downside of Deciding style, one that she perceived as being closed to new ideas and obsessed with efficient goal achievement. What Ellie had failed to realize is that by seeing only the downside of the Deciding style, she missed out on the upside: setting goals and priorities, evaluating ideas and solutions, and committing to one course of action. She had lost a valuable resource and a source of creativity and power.

Once she committed to developing her flexibility by using the Deciding style, Ellie began to connect with the style's upside and the difference it could make in her own effectiveness. Ellie could not fully express the Deciding style right away because it was so unfamiliar; instead, she approached the task creatively by using her preferred Imagining style. She devised experiments that allowed her to discern, approximate, and hone intentionally. With more practice, Ellie was able to add Deciding style skills—firmly committing, critically evaluating, and objectively judging—to her repertoire.

Sharma and Kolb found that people who prefer the abstract styles of Reflecting, Analyzing, and Thinking and work in professions that require science and math competence (engineering, medicine, and law, for instance) seem to have more difficulty building flexibility than those people with styles of Initiating, Experiencing and Imagining.[1] Due to situational demands and learning style preference, individuals with abstract learning styles become entrenched in the scientific problem-solving mentality and find it difficult to build the concrete, feeling-oriented, and active skills associated with concrete learning styles. Kolb and Wolf found engineers often experienced difficulty moving from the role of individual contributors, which allows them to focus on the strengths of their learning styles, to the role of manager or leader, which requires them to flex to other styles. Many engineers reported feeling underqualified for their managerial role.[2]

If you are strongly tied to a specialized learning style, it helps to connect with the upside of the style you are seeking. Do you avoid speaking in front of groups? Just imagine if you could communicate with ease. Do you shy away from difficult conversations with your colleagues? Think how you could prevent upset feelings if you could initiate those discussions. When you connect with the benefits of the style you are trying to develop and recognize that your own learning style has a downside, too, you introduce a catalyst for the learning process.

You may find that developing a nonpreferred style can be like picking up a slippery fish—it's is difficult to capture on one try. The deeper you are attached to your own style, the more unfamiliar the opposite style becomes, so developing the capabilities of that style requires learning over time. Actively trying to build strengths in a new learning style is half of the equation; try also to contain and minimize the inhibiting effects of your preferred learning style on the style that you are trying to express.

Developing the capacity for Experiencing. Experiencing requires fully opening yourself to the present moment and paying attention to your feelings without worrying about what they mean. Meditating and focusing are two means of developing experiencing skills. Overthinking an experience can inhibit your ability to directly sense and feel the immediate moment. This presence and attention are particularly important for building relationships, leading a team, managing emotions, and being present to others.

Developing the capacity for Imagining. Imagining requires both contemplating experiences and reflecting on them to consider a wide range of options. Judging too quickly can inhibit your ability to use the Imagining style. Seeking the opinions of others and keeping a curious mind are important for generating new ideas and being comfortable in ambiguous situations.

Developing the capacity for Reflecting. Reflecting requires space and time. Impulsive desires and pressures to take action can inhibit reflection. You can enhance your ability to reflect by deliberately viewing things from different perspectives and striving to feel empathy. Meditating can also foster deep reflection. Gathering and making sense of information can help you develop the Reflecting learning style.

Developing the capacity for Analyzing. Analyzing requires both logical thinking and reflection to organize information and create a plan. An extreme focus on details enhances Analyzing, but diversion and interruptions inhibit your ability to analyze. Coming up with theories, analyzing data, and integrating information to get the full picture can help you to develop the Analyzing learning style.

Developing the capacity for Thinking. Thinking requires the ability to represent and manipulate ideas in your head. Intense emotion and sensations or pressure to act quickly can disrupt the thinking process. Engagement in thinking can be enhanced by creating scenarios for action. Using numbers to analyze problems, making independent judgments, and framing arguments with logic can also aid in the development and expression of the Thinking learning style.

Developing the capacity for Deciding. Deciding requires making an independent judgment through thinking and committing to one course of practical action. Ambiguity and remaining open to new ideas can inhibit deciding. Determining standards of success and measuring your progress toward that goal develops the Deciding style.

Developing the capacity for Acting. Acting requires commitment and involvement in the practical world of real consequences. Acting brings the first previous learning styles of Experiencing, Imagining, Reflecting, Analyzing, Thinking, and Deciding and tests them in reality. Spending too much time in the other learning styles can inhibit Acting. Checklists, timetables, and taking even a small action toward a goal can help you develop the Acting style.

Developing the capacity for Initiating. Initiating requires trial and error based on feelings to seize new opportunities. Too much analysis inhibits Initiating, while bouncing back from temporary setbacks and motivating others enhance Initiating. Improvisation, positive thinking, and redefining your definition of failure can help you develop the Initiating style.

Developing the Balancing style. Balancing requires moving between acting, reflecting, feeling, and thinking as the situation demands. A strong adherence to one specialized learning style inhibits the Balancing style. Uncovering blind spots and adapting to people and situations can help you develop the Balancing style.

Table 4.2 lists questions that people tend to ask themselves when using each learning style. You can use these questions to guide your learning process when trying to adopt an unfamiliar style.

Initiating	Experiencing	Imagining
■ What action should I take now? ■ How do I start? ■ Where are the next opportunities? ■ Can I take a chance on this? ■ How can I motivate others?	■ Am I experiencing the issue in the present? ■ What is my intuition telling me? ■ What am I feeling? ■ Where is my attention now? ■ Am I engaged?	■ What are the possibilities? ■ What is my vision? ■ How do I feel about this situation? ■ What do others think? ■ What do I imagine will happen?
Acting	**Balancing**	**Reflecting**
■ How can I implement this plan? ■ How much time do I have? ■ What resources do I need? ■ What are the next steps? ■ Who can help me make progress?	■ Is there a blind spot? ■ Have I considered all possibilities? ■ Do I need to change my approach?	■ What is another way of looking at this? ■ What are my assumptions? ■ What information is most meaningful? ■ What else do I need to consider?
Deciding	**Thinking**	**Analyzing**
■ What is my goal? ■ What is the cost to benefit? ■ What is the bottom line? ■ What is my decision? ■ What is the most practical solution? ■ What is working or not working?	■ Am I being objective? ■ What do the numbers tell me? ■ Am I accurate and thorough? ■ Have I put my feelings aside? ■ Is this a logical approach?	■ What is my plan? ■ Can I create a scenario about what will happen? ■ How can I minimize mistakes? ■ Is my reasoning conceptually sound? ■ What processes will support consistency?

Table 4.2 Questions to Guide Adoption of Learning Styles.

Embodying Your Style

Learning styles are deeply engrained; they are evident not just in how you think but also in how you feel, perceive, and behave—even in your gestures, posture, and movements. Building awareness about your own learning flexibility can be elusive, but you can use your physical behavior to gain insight into your learning style. Physical flexibility may provide a way for you to gauge your general flexibility in life and learning, too. People generally embody their learning style by moving in ways that are characteristic of the skills and attitudes of the learning style they favor. After all, an individual who gravitates toward the Acting style will need be quicker, stronger, and more free-flowing in movement than someone who spends more time in the Reflecting style, where the movements are more minimal, sustained, and controlled.

For example, Lance, an accountant, prefers the Analyzing style. Lance spends most of his day sitting behind his computer, crunching numbers for his clients. In fact, once he paid attention to his movements over the course of a day, he found that he was in only a few positions for about eighty percent of his day. Lance sits in a chair facing forward—typically with his right leg crossed over his left leg and his arms narrowly reaching out to his keyboard. He keeps his lower back rigidly straight and his shoulders slumped forward. His movements are slow and controlled; in fact, he often keeps his body in the same position for minutes at a time and senses tension in his shoulders. His vision is focused intently on the computer screen. His breath is shallow and high in his chest. At least three days per week, Lance enjoys running to get exercise. When he runs, his movements are rhythmical and repetitive in a front-to-back motion. Lance rarely moves from side to side or in ways that require a twist at the waist. He recognizes that it has been a long time since he moved with any free, easy spontaneity like he might have as a child on the playground. Like most adults, Lance spends so much time doing the same things everyday in habitual activities that his movements are habitual, too. He might even find that he only moves in about ten different ways on a regular basis, unlike young children who move in hundreds of ways.

Your own flexibility—in life and learning—may be evident through your own movements. Are you typically loose and relaxed, or more controlled with some tension? Do you make your body narrow by crossing your arms and legs, or are your shoulders wide and arms open? Understanding your movement preferences—your postures, gestures, tension levels, and even the way you breathe—can change the way you experience the world and the impact you have on others.

To explore various movement styles, you may want to watch other people and compare their movements to your own. As you experiment with different forms of movement styles, notice which ones are comfortable and which feel foreign. When you build flexibility with your body by moving in different ways, you also build learning flexibility by creating an experience of standing in the space of new styles. To learn more about how learning styles are embodied, see the Style Sheets in Appendix B.

Challenging Yourself

Think of one thing you would like to change in yourself that is most critical for your success—just one, no matter how small. Find a highly motivating self-development goal that will help you make that change. This may be a quality or capability that you would like to acquire. For instance, do you need to become more attuned to relationships, more practical, or more analytical? It may be a strength that is overplayed or a weakness that holds you back. This will be a goal that increases your flexibility to use a learning style that is not as familiar to you. This one step will be the beginning of a lifelong quest to increase your ability to use all nine ways of learning. When you feel stuck in a rut, being aware of your preferences and broadening your comfort zone will help you see new possibilities toward greater flexibility, capability, and success.

Learning flexibility and mobility within the learning cycle are antidotes for the inflexibility of a single specialized learning style. The more you can incorporate the nine learning styles, the more flexibility you will develop and the more freedom and confidence you will have in meeting situations as they arise. You will be better prepared for challenges and transitions if you have the response range that learning flexibility provides. Learning flexibility also sets you up to manage the inevitable challenges of adult life including that of specialization, the topic of the next chapter.

Learning Flexibility Checklist for Action

When developing learning flexibility, you may find it easiest to add one style at a time to your repertoire. Follow these steps to get started:

• Choose one learning style that will up your game.

• Using the Style Sheets in Appendix B of this book, identify the capabilities that are expressed in that style.

• Using the learning cycle as a guide, begin to learn how to use that style. Be mindful of experiences, imagine new possibilities and benefits, reflect to make sense and take perspectives, analyze to create a plan, think to use general concepts and facts, decide on a goal, try new behaviors, and seek feedback regarding your progress. Begin again. Monitor your progress toward your goal.

• Enlist help from others who will be supportive. Tell them of your learning goal and ask that they hold you accountable.

Practice Using Learning Flexibility

Think of a situation in your life where you are currently learning or a project that you are currently working on. It could be, for example, a career or relationship challenge, a project, activity, or event you are planning; or a new hobby that you are starting.

Now Follow These Steps:

1. On a blank sheet of paper draw a large grid to create the nine learning styles like the one in Figure 3.2.

2. Decide which learning style or styles you are using in your current project or learning situation.

3. In each part of the grid, write some notes to capture how you are applying your chosen learning style(s) to your project or situation.

4. Next, using the questions below as a guide, jot down other approaches you might take to enhance your learning.

    • Am I using only my preferred learning style(s)?

    • Am I moving around the learning cycle and using learning styles that are not typical for me, or am I staying close to my preferred learning style(s)?

    • What difficulties am I encountering in using other learning styles?

    • When I look at things from the perspective of different learning styles, how does it change my understanding of my project or learning situation? Does it reveal other factors or issues that I can address?

• What can I do to increase my ability to use different learning styles?

* What three things can I start doing?

* What three things should I stop doing?

* What three things can I do differently?

Reflection on Using Learning Flexibility

You may find it helpful to journal about your use of the learning cycle. Below you will find prompts for your reflections.

• Consider a situation that you have recently encountered. Use the following questions to assess your ability to use all the learning styles:

* Which styles are most comfortable for me?

* What do I gain from using these preferred styles?

* What do I give up when using only these styles?

* Which learning styles do I seem to avoid using?

* What do I gain from avoiding these nonpreferred styles?

What do I give up by avoiding these styles?

- Which learning styles would I like to use more often? Why?

    * Does my learning flexibility profile match my self-assessment?

    * Draw a mind map based on Flexibility. The center of the map would be "My Goals for Increasing Flexibility."

Chapter Five

Learning Flexibility and the Road Ahead

Live as if you were to die tomorrow. Learn as if you were to live forever.

Mahatma Gandhi

A human being should be able to change a diaper, plan an invasion, butcher a hog, conn a ship, design a building, write a sonnet, balance accounts, build a wall, set a bone, comfort the dying, take orders, give orders, cooperate, act alone, pitch manure, solve equations, analyze a new problem, program a computer, cook a tasty meal, fight efficiently, die gallantly. Specialization is for insects.

Robert Heinlein

In our early years, most of us search for a career that fits our interests and talents: a path where we find a niche in our life situation so we can contribute, make a living, and find satisfaction. When we find that path, we tend to specialize and develop the characteristics that will make us successful. We develop a learning style that meets the challenges of our career choice and helps us master what we need to succeed. As we gain experience in our field and mature, the road ahead becomes broader and more complex with more challenges and choices that require different learning styles than our specialized style. It is here where developing learning flexibility and the skills and capabilities of other learning styles can enhance lifelong learning, success, and fulfillment.

This chapter explains how a strong learning style preference can help you to perfect your skills and create a comfort zone and shows how to avoid getting stuck in a rut. Learning flexibility helps you stay on course to make the learning way your approach to life. Learning flexibility can enable you to take full advantage of the full cycle learning as you face the challenges of the many transitions ahead of you in life—perfecting your special skill, rising to greater responsibility, changing career, finding a work/life balance, expressing your total self, and serving a greater purpose.

Why Do We Get in a Rut?

In almost everything, we play to our strengths—sports, friendships, home life, careers. Why wouldn't we? Over time, strengths we overuse may become weaknesses. Since we tend to prefer one or two of the learning styles, the effectiveness of our learning style is limited to those situations that require its strengths and capabilities. Our knowledge and interests tend to relate to our area of specialization at the expense of other areas of our lives. We focus on our interests, paying more and more attention to them, while avoiding activities or experiences that we are not interested in or that we feel unskilled in. The well-worn pathways of our learning preferences are reinforced when we enter a field of specialization that allows us to seek the experiences that make use of our learning style. However, when we become entrenched in our preferences, we miss out on other possibilities. Being entrenched is like riding a bike in a well-worn rut. We move forward without the ability to steer the bike. But when we are aware of our preferences and able to use the other learning styles, we are more capable of responding to new situations with the learning style that is a match for the situation. Over time, this allows us to gain new strengths and capabilities that can transform our lives. This is more like riding a bike on a wide, open path; we can steer to keep our options open and respond to whatever challenges may arise.

Perfecting Your Special Skill: Beginning Your Career

As you begin your career, you will be well served to play to your strengths. This will help you to choose situations in which you can be successful. Pay attention to what interests you by using the Experiencing style to connect with your feelings about what you enjoy doing. Then use the Imagining style to generate many ideas about how your interests might translate into job activities, and use the Reflecting style to determine how these job activities might come together in a career. After you have identified a possible career path, you can use the Analyzing style to make a plan for looking into that career, the Thinking style to define your existing skills and your educational strategy for acquiring any skills you might need, and the Deciding style to commit to one course of action, however small, toward pursuing this career. Using the Acting style, try out a class, event, or volunteer opportunity that allows you to experience the career path, and then use the Initiating style to seek new opportunities to build and refine your experience.

The more you are able to use this learning cycle process to examine and develop your interests, the clearer your capabilities and career choice will become.

As you continue to build your capabilities within your chosen field, you will be called upon to become more flexible. For instance, a physician who prefers the Deciding style ultimately will need to work on teams, requiring more Experiencing and Imagining capabilities. A social worker who prefers the Imagining style will need to hone his skills in budgeting and strategy as he runs a department or writes a grant. Focus on your strengths at first and build flexibility along the way.

Remaining Specialized for your Entire Career?

Specialization is a necessary foundation in the developmental process, and most adults seem to find a comfortable niche within their field. Many professionals have built a satisfying life around their specialized preference. They find that they are comfortable and successful in their specialized role. Betsy, for example, used her Reflecting style preference to follow a career in academia. As a university professor, she focused on one field of study that provided tremendous personal fulfillment with time to conduct research and to write. She built learning flexibility to allow her to manage situations that arose within the structured, satisfying life she created.

If you are one of the fortunate few in today's world who has found a long-term specialized career where your specialized learning style serves you well, you may still discover that you need other learning styles in order to perform at the highest level in your work. In the previous chapter we saw numerous examples of how people's ability to flex to different learning styles enhanced and supported their performance, creativity, and life satisfaction.

Most people find that toward mid-career and beyond, life becomes more complex as career roles evolve, challenges arise, and opportunities present themselves that demand a different approach. These tensions press individuals to navigate the learning cycle in different, creative ways, choosing between the pairs of opposite styles. Over time, developing strengths in all of the learning modes is the strongest approach to resolving a dilemma. Most of us, however, are in the process of reaching that goal and thus approach life with some combination of our preferred learning style and a few of the other learning ways.

A focus on learning will eventually allow you to make life a continuous *process* of learning rather than worrying only about learning *content.* You will increase your awareness, have a more sophisticated grasp of the world, and manage yourself in a highly creative way. What might not be immediately evident is that these shifts also make your life richer and expand your potential. So while no universities teach adults how to continue maturing, the learning way is the key to full development and to facing life's challenges.

Rising to Greater Responsibility: Learning to Develop

As a new associate, Martina practiced law under the direction of a partner at her law firm. As she continued her career, she discovered that her professional role extended beyond providing expertise, and it was a stretch for her Analyzing style preference. When Martina became a partner at her law firm, she realized that she was essentially running her own business within the context of the firm. Her roles extended from the practice of law to include the business of law. She was called on not only to provide direct legal work but also to include client relations, business development, staff development, strategy formulation, and leading collaborative teams. As Martina moved forward in her career, she experienced a transition in which the increasing demands of her job required a more holistic approach and a greater repertoire of capabilities. She had expected to complete her career without veering from the role that came naturally.

Martina preferred her comfortable role of providing direct legal service; however, she recognized that lawyers no longer have that luxury of clinging to their favorite roles. Now, as in any highly competitive and entrepreneurial situation, law firm partners must possess capabilities to assume all roles. In order to transition successfully, Martina needed to learn from experience.

Professionals move from the specialized learning style they use early in their careers to a more integrated, flexible approach later in their professional lives. This integration is only realized if they decide to meet the challenge by developing new capabilities. A mature professional is called upon to use a complex set of skills and fill many roles that focus on clients and content, meaning, and outcome. Building a repertoire of capabilities and roles requires a learning attitude that can be difficult for specialists who have become successful from excelling in a particular field.

Each learning style represents a partial set of your capabilities. By understanding your learning style, you have an overview of your current strengths and capabilities, a clear description of the styles you have yet to develop, and a map for your professional growth.

The path of integration depends upon your dominant and nonexpressed learning preferences. If you have a Thinking preference, you will shift your focus to the Experiencing style emphasizing emotions, relationships, and sensory experience. If you prefer a Reflecting style, you will shift toward Acting by taking charge, initiating change, and taking new risks. When you shift your perspective to the nondominant learning ones you may have previously repressed, you will begin to experience yourself as a *process.* The new way you navigate the learning cycle using a nondominant style can change your self-identity.

Returning to the example of Martina: once she began to shift her orientation on the learning cycle, she experienced situations as well as herself in an entirely new way. She explains:

I used to scan for problems and react. When something would go wrong, I looked for people to blame just like I had been blamed as I was coming up in the ranks. It's all I knew how to do. But, my partner was the best role model I could have imagined. He never got rattled or reactive; he never lost his cool when situations were tense. Instead of blaming others or blowing up, he became creative and brought out the best in all of us. He always seemed to get better results in the long run. When I took on leadership positions, I started practicing his approach. My learning style preference is Thinking, so it took time to use the Experiencing style and to become more reflective especially when I wanted to (over) react. As I gained more experience from sticking with some uncomfortable moments, I began to see those situations as opportunities to become more creative in my responses. At times, I could slow down these situations, which gave me time to process. Now I can observe when others are caught in automatic reactions. I feel so relieved that I have overcome those habitual responses. I have a different perception of myself because of this experience.

When Martina expanded her specialized Thinking approach to incorporate the Experiencing, Imagining, and Reflecting styles in her own unique way, she was able to connect with others, imagine different possibilities, and pause to allow situations to settle, even in the most trying times. She found that her ability to use the other learning styles in authentic ways changed the way she approached the Thinking style, too. She was less compelled to disconnect and to become dispassionate. She was able to reflect back on her previous behavior and recognize that she had believed there was only one right way to do things, though now she could see a vast array of possibilities. After developing new learning capabilities, Martina was no longer hostage to this rigid belief. She was learning new and more sophisticated ways of feeling, perceiving, thinking, and acting.

Creating a Second Act: Transitions and Career Change

Change is beyond our control; it happens whether or not we are prepared for it. Transitions, on the other hand, are situations that require us to reorient and redefine ourselves. An adaptive and flexible approach toward lifelong learning can guide us in intentionally adjusting to transitions with resilience, openness, and courage. The learning way allows us to manage transitions by continually learning from our own experiences, understanding our own unique style, and creating a learning-based strategy to transform ourselves while we are adapting to changing circumstances.

William Bridges, the renowned expert on transitions, identified three phases in any transition: the end of one period, the neutral zone, and the new beginning.[1] Li experienced these three phases as he adapted to losing his job as a financial analyst through downsizing after a merger. He used the steps in the learning cycle to guide him through each phase.

At the end of the first stage, the ending, he intentionally used the Experiencing style to connect with his own feelings of vulnerability and fear as he processed the knowledge that his job would be eliminated. Li's typical response would have been to withdraw and deal with the situation in a solitary fashion. Instead, he connected not only with his own values but also with others in the same situation in the Imagining style before making sense of the situation in the Reflecting style. In the Analyzing style, he created a plan to organize all the information he would need to consider before deciding what to do next. This plan allowed him to make some independent judgments about the financial implications of his situation in the Thinking style. Li used the Deciding style to commit to saying goodbye to all of the people in his department before his departure. In the Acting style, he implemented his transition plan before using the Initiating style to enter the next phase of his life with optimism.

While in the neutral zone, Li approached learning with a different emphasis. Because he had so much more life experience than when he had first chosen his career in finance, he knew that he would need to reconnect with his feelings and intuition. Initially he focused more on *being* than *doing.* He spent time in quiet reflection to connect with his deepest desires and fears. He created a personal vision that included the values that guide him and his greatest hopes for the future. This took time alone and time in conversation with trusted advisors, family, and close friends. Also, he reflected on the parts of his life he would want to keep the same and those he would want to change.

As he took his time, new ideas began to emerge. Li recognized that he had entered his current career more out of a need for a stable income than for any innate interest. He had quelled his interest in the field of human resources that seemed too soft to ensure that he would always have a job. Li discovered that he most enjoyed his career when he was coaching and mentoring new employees in his department. He realized that while he understood the principles of financial analysis, such as what made for a good investment, he did not know much about the process of coaching. As he investigated the field, he found that the specialty of retirement coaching was emerging in response to the number of baby boomers. Although this involved more than simply looking at finances, Li was drawn to the field for its holistic approach.

As he moved toward action, Li became discouraged as he looked at his strengths, weaknesses, education, and experience. He compared his current reality to what he would need to tackle this new interest. Li decided that he could not make the career transition immediately or in one step. It was too risky since he needed to pay his mortgage and college tuition for his daughter. He did, however, commit to a timetable that would allow him to measure his progress against his goal: within eighteen months, he would complete his retirement coaching program and log enough hours to achieve his certification before launching his own business. As Li implemented his plan, he found that he approached life with new purpose.

Li continued to spiral around the learning cycle as he learned his way through his transition. Although Li made some alterations to his plan as he gained more information by trial and error, within two years of leaving his position in financial services, he was situated in his new career.

Work/Life Balance: Making Work and Life One

Becoming an expert can have the unintended consequence of creating a limited sense of self and an unbalanced life. Professionals rise to the peak of their field by perfecting their specialized skills in a work environment that is competitive and oriented toward rewarding individual achievement. However, an integrated, balanced life is holistic, involving more collaboration than competition.

Erik Dane suggests that when experts are faced with dynamic, unpredictable conditions within their area of expertise, they increase their flexibility to remain open to possibilities, information, and options for action. He recommends that experts deliberately focus some of their attention outside their specialized field to find "doubt-inducing exceptions" to their beliefs about the best approach for their work. He points out that doubt is often considered an important element of wisdom. This doubt functions not to reduce experts' confidence but to build their flexibility by helping them question their own habits, use their creativity, and seek out additional challenging experiences.[2]

In addition to developing flexibility at work, we must strive to create balance between work and life, applying the same vitality and energy we bring to our careers to all areas of our lives. The balance between body and mind is important, particularly when our physical health becomes an issue or when our work is stressful or mentally taxing. Often we must break the confines of the technological, fast-paced, civilized world and reestablish our connection with the organic beauty of the natural world in order to feel balanced. As we expand our specialized learning style, becoming more flexible in our approach to learning and appreciating those with different learning styles, we can establish a sense of centeredness and balance as we understand how the different parts of the cycle make up the whole. Seeking balance through the learning cycle frees us from implicit assumptions and opens new possibilities and perspectives.

Logan, a financial analyst who preferred the Reflecting style, found that his learning style was a good fit for his career. His preference didn't work as well for parenting. When with his two-year-old son, Logan recognized that he spent time passively watching him instead of actively playing. Next time they went to the playground, Logan recognized this tendency to sit on a bench observing. To his amazement, he reported that he could use learning style flexibility to help him improve his own and his son's experience. He said,

I started with the Acting and Initiating styles by playing with my son Aiden. I got up and pushed him on the swing. I don't know why it never dawned on me to do that before when I have been at the playground with him. I used Experiencing to stay engaged and present—not to think about the past or the future—just to pay attention to being with my son. I felt this incredible love for my son as I hugged him when he got off the swing. I used the Thinking style to remember what children of his age should be able to do by themselves. Finally, I went back to my Reflecting style to watch Aiden playing. As I did, I was amazed at how paying attention to the other learning styles added to my experience and helped me learn about myself.

As Logan was able to integrate other styles in his parenting approach, he also gained confidence that he could practice them at work, too. Eventually, Logan's facility with other learning styles even helped him to use the Reflecting style intentionally when he believed the situation called for that style. His ability to build learning flexibility helped him to create a whole, balanced life that brought him happiness on every front.

Expressing Your Total Self

Many of us have focused our attention and energy on building a life around our chosen interest. When you do this, you may begin to define yourself by what you know or do. You may be among the many professionals who specialized early by becoming a physician, engineer, nurse, lawyer, manager, educator, accountant, or social worker. The life of a professional can be comfortable, secure, and fulfilling. It provides job security, but the defined demands of the role can ultimately thwart your ability to fulfill your own needs. Recognizing this inherent conflict triggers a need for learning flexibility and the ability to integrate all the learning styles. You may recognize this need gradually, or it may happen in an instant as a result of a crisis such as divorce or job loss. For others, the need may fade into the background because they are so entrenched in their current life and lifestyle. It's simply too disruptive to respond to the conflict.

If you use a Thinking preference, the shift brings a new focus on the Experiencing style with emphasis on emotions, relationships, and sensory experience. If you have primarily used the Reflecting style, you will shift toward the Acting style by taking charge, initiating change, and taking new risks. When you are able to shift your perspective by integrating the nondominant styles of learning that you have previously ignored, you begin to experience yourself as a *process.* The new way in which you navigate the learning cycle using the nondominant style can even change your self-identity.

What are the benefits of this integrated life? You will both adapt to and create your own life situation by changing your situation as you see fit and letting your experiences change you. Brazilian educator Paulo Freire noted that in order to change you must feel like the director of your own life, the "subject" instead of the "object."[3]

People who have integrated their preferred and nonpreferred ways of learning find that they become more capable and mature. They do not allow what is typical to dictate what is possible. Nora provides an example. Living in a small town, Nora found that she did not initially miss her career in nursing as she easily fell into life as a professional's wife. While her husband carried on his surgical practice, she focused on her home, children, and community volunteerism. She relied on her Experiencing, Imagining, and Reflecting preferences to be present, to help others, and to be patient. These styles also helped her to work well on teams, inspiring others to imagine new possibilities for the community. Nora recognized that she was skilled at working interdependently with others; however, she was not as familiar at being independent in thoughts or actions. Once her children were away at college, Nora began to pay attention to learning more about herself and her own needs. This meant that she had to build capabilities in the Thinking way to separate from the present moment.

She had to build her ability to use the Deciding way to firmly commit to what was important to her. And, because independence is impossible without taking action, Nora had to learn to behave in ways that allowed her to express her own uniqueness.

Over the course of the next few years, Nora found that she could tap her abilities to be both interdependent and independent. Her life became full of variety and diversity. By building capabilities in learning styles that were opposite to her preferred style, she had integrated her ability to use all the styles in a unique, creative way. She had balanced and integrated all parts of life and all parts of herself. Even though she experienced change and even stress, she seemed to experience less turbulence than she would have previously. Her experience in managing the tension of her dilemma of independence-interdependence had helped her to manage other tensions that often cause conflict and drama for others.

Serving a Greater Purpose

In the first part of our lives, we are primarily concerned with finding ourselves, establishng our identity, and achieving independence, competence, and success. The preoccupation with ourselves can be especially intense in individualistic cultures like the United States. Maturity gives rise to empathy and an urge to care for others, usually first within our families and later in the wider community and the world at large. With increasing competence and power there comes the responsibility to contribute more to the greater good.

Empathy and caring for others brings a powerful sense of purpose and meaning. When we contribute to the success of others, our work outlasts the span of our own lives. Caring also means careful work that ensures quality in the services and products we provide others.

Mark was an expert when it came to personal career achievements. He was a successful, top-grossing salesperson preparing to take over the sales and marketing helm for his employer. As he crafted his strategy to make his mark, he looked back at his own career. He was aware that he often acted in self-interest by prompting customers to make short-term decisions that benefited his sales quotas rather than paying attention to what was in their best interests. In fact, he had even fought management when they proposed giving a percentage of profits back to the communities they served because it would impact his bonus. As he accepted responsibility in his new role, he wondered how could he make changes that would express more care for his employees, the work of his department, and his customers. He thought about how investments in the community could make a difference in so many lives both within and outside his company.

Mark was experiencing the challenge of *generativity:* the ability to enact change. As he accepted responsibility for the organization, he was also given the power to transform it. He grappled with how to care for relationships, how to encourage careful work, and how to use his power to provide leadership while still caring for himself. Mark used the Imagining style to identify his values and the values of his colleagues. In the Reflecting style he took many perspectives, trying to make sense of how he could use this information to begin to change.

Mark included the Analyzing style to structure policies that promoted ethical practices and institutionalized new ways of working to benefit everyone in the company. Mark wanted to be logical as he approached this challenge, so he carefully analyzed the quantitative data that supported his decisions. He would not be showing care for others if he made hasty decisions that jeopardized the business in the long term. Mark found that the Deciding style allowed him to identify the most beneficial investment for employees: training and development. He also made sure to identify a way to measure their success in delivering these programs.

Mark used the Acting style to implement his plans to take care of himself and others. One way he did this was to incorporate daily exercise into his routine. He served as a role model for others when he held "walking meetings" with colleagues so that they could get some exercise and conduct their business simultaneously. Mark continued to seek new opportunities to serve a greater purpose. In doing so, he practiced the Initiating style.

The learning way has broader implications than career—it applies to all life situations. Specializing in one style can be beneficial at times, but an overreliance on that style ultimately limits your ability to achieve learning flexibility and to benefit from all of the steps in the learning process. To build flexibility, you need to practice the learning cycle every day. The next chapter focuses on strategies you can use to incorporate the learning way into your life.

Checklist

Determine how your learning flexibility is supporting or challenging you in your current situation.

Reflection

You may find it helpful to journal about your use of learning flexibility in your current life situation. Below you will find prompts for your reflections.

- Consider your career path. Did you play to your specialized strengths or adapt to skills that were not your preference?

- What are your nondominant styles? What capabilities will you gain when you develop flexibility in these styles?

- If you specialized in your career, have you remained specialized or built your learning style flexibility? What are the benefits and challenges of your choice?

- Do you hold back from participating in certain types of situations? Are you in a rut in any part of your life?

Chapter Six

What's Next? Deliberate Learning for Life

I believe that we learn by practice. Whether it means to learn to dance by practicing dancing or to learn to live by practicing living, the principles are the same. In each, it is the performance of a dedicated precise set of acts, physical or intellectual, from which comes shape of achievement, a sense of one's being, a satisfaction of spirit. One becomes, in some area, an athlete of God. Practice means to perform, over and over again in the face of all obstacles, some act of vision, of faith, of desire. Practice is a means of inviting the perfection desired.

Martha Graham

How do you put the essentials of the learning way into practice? This chapter covers three strategies to help you to build learning flexibility and ultimately transform your life: deep experiencing, deliberate learning, and starting small with one big thing. By intentionally integrating your quest for learning flexibility into your daily life, you will continue to follow a path of self-discovery. This path reveals itself in the moment, presenting new challenges and opportunities to unleash the hidden parts of yourself as you travel down it step by step.

Practice Deep Experiencing

We have described experiencing as the gateway to learning. It is not *experience,* but *experiencing* that is the source of learning. Because of our habits and stereotypes, we live through many experiences without actually experiencing them. John Dewey believed that to initiate reflection and learning our habitual experience must be interrupted by deep experiencing, such as when we are stuck with a problem or difficulty or struck by the strangeness of something outside of our usual experience.[1] But we can also strip our biases from our experiences in more deliberate ways.

Mindfulness. The practice of mindfulness aims to overcome habitual thinking and to reach direct, pure experience through mindful awareness and attention. Mindfulness is the core of Buddhist meditation, the discipline of anchoring the mind in the present moment. This is often accompanied with a practice of awareness and acceptance through breathing. Jon Kabat-Zinn, Professor of Medicine Emeritus and creator of the Stress Reduction Clinic and the Center for Mindfulness in Medicine, Health Care, and Society at the University of Massachusetts Medical School, defines mindfulness as "paying attention in a particular way—on purpose, in the present moment and non-judgmentally."[2] Nonjudgment, in mindfulness theory, is accepting the current state as part of a constant flow of changing experiences. This theory suggests that letting go of judgment strengthens the mind, and it challenges the illusion that we can control our experiences by overthinking them. We often find ourselves responding to situations automatically, without questioning our habits, as if we are only half awake. Mindfulness helps us wake up to the present moment, experience it more vividly, and react to it in more intentional ways.

To practice mindfulness, you can start by drawing your attention to your five senses. This helps anchor you in the present moment. Then you can begin to focus on your breathing, gradually slowing it down. With practice, mindfulness can help quiet the mind and reduce automatic, habitual patterns of thinking and responding. This presence enhances direct concrete experience and allows the learning cycle to begin. In a sense, we cannot learn from experience if we do not first *have* an experience; often, automatic routines distract us from experiencing the moment.

Intentional attention. Being aware of what we pay attention to can help us consciously create our experience. Mindfulness practice can help us consider how we choose to process and learn from the events in our lives. By intentionally guiding the learning process and paying attention to how we are going through the phases of the learning cycle, we create ourselves through learning. We are what we learn. How and what we learn determines the way we process the possibilities of each new emerging experience, which in turn determines the range of choices and decisions we see. The choices and decisions we make, to some extent, determine the events we live through, and these events influence our future choices. Thus, we create ourselves by choosing what we pay attention to and how we process and respond to that experience. For many, this learning choice is relatively unconscious, an autopilot program for learning. Mindfulness can pave the way for us to control our learning and our life through intentional attention.

To practice intentional attention, begin by becoming aware of your body sensation. How are you feeling in any moment? What do you notice about your own reactions?

Focusing. Research in the field of psychotherapy has shown that the more patients are able to experience deeply, the better the outcome of their therapy. Carl Rogers proposed that when patients learn to appreciate different aspects of themselves, become aware of their changing feelings, and trust in their process of experiencing, they realize that they can change their way of thinking or choose to approach problems in a new way.[3] The philosopher Eugene Gendlin, who worked with Rogers, called this deep experiencing ability "focusing," and he believed that the physical sensations of our bodies play a role in our ability to experience the present moment.[4] When we become aware of shifts in our bodily sensations, we can analyze these shifts and interpret them.

Like mindfulness and intentional attention, focusing emphasizes awareness in the present moment. Some Buddhist practitioners use the focusing technique to complement their meditative practices. Unlike mindfulness and intentional attention, which are primarily solitary practices, focusing benefits from someone guiding us through the steps of the focusing process. However, we can also learn to guide ourselves through the process.

In his book *Focusing,* Gendlin developed a basic six-step technique for learning how to engage in this kind of direct body experiencing. The first step involves making time for the activity in a *safe and quiet space* and then focusing your attention inward on your body sensations. Next, think about a problem or challenge you are currently facing and pay attention to the sensation that arises when you focus on that problem. This sensation is *felt sense.* Pay attention until you sense what the unclear problem feels like. Then find a word or phrase that describes the felt sense, going back and forth between the felt sense and various words and phrases until one resonates. Next, ask yourself, "What is the whole problem that makes this felt sense?" Does the problem you are facing have several aspects? Is the root of the problem related to a deeper issue? Asking yourself about a specific conflict you are having with a coworker, for example, might reveal a deeper problem about your overall satisfaction with your professional role.

Try out answers until one fits and creates a sense of release. Finally *receive* the release by reflecting on it for a few moments.[5]

Make Learning Deliberate

While the practices in the book will help you to improve your performance or learn new content, the goal is to pay attention to your own learning process and to become more flexible in managing it. This process is what allows you to transform your life. Deliberate learning requires that you understand your unique way of learning from experience and use it to intentionally direct and control your behavior. Instead of being locked into an unconscious force that operates in the background and guides you automatically, you can use the learning cycle as a guide to help you learn deliberately. The learning way literally changes your mind, allowing you to process and respond to your experiences differently.

To learn deliberately, you first need to become a witness of your own process. *Zoom out* from your automatic response—the learning style that you prefer—and question whether that style might be limiting what you see as possible. Where could you shift on the learning cycle to increase your effectiveness? Next, choose the learning style that is the best match for your situation and *zoom in* to use it. This will create a new experience, and the cycle continues again.

Lynne's favored style of Deciding meant that her go-to response for any situation allowed her to critically evaluate a situation and commit to a solution. Because she had easy access to the Acting and Initiating styles too, she was quick to implement a practical fix to a problem. This command-and-control approach had made her successful as a director in a health-care organization and carried over to the way she ran her home and raised her kids. As Lynne developed her learning flexibility and the ability to evaluate her process of learning, she recognized that this approach was not the best match with her twenty-year-old daughter Danielle.

One night, when Danielle arrived home from college upset from something that had happened, Lynne stopped herself from leading with her automatic Deciding style. She zoomed out to witness where she was on the learning cycle versus where the best match for the situation might be. Lynne actually used the quick processing of her Deciding style to choose the opposite styles of learning in the moment: Experiencing, Imagining, and Reflecting. In uncharacteristic fashion, Lynne did not try to diagnose or fix a problem. She simply sat down, connected with her daughter through her presence, and listened. Instead of tapping her problem-solving prowess, she tapped into her empathy. Danielle said that she had never felt more heard or understood. When Lynne shifted her approach to learning in the moment by zooming out to see what was needed, she increased her effectiveness with her daughter and learned about herself in the process. The intentional process is key.

Learning how to learn is a lifelong process. The 10,000 hours that some say is required to master a skill may be a mythical number, but the number of learning cycles we go through in our lifetime is countless. Being deliberate about the learning process can improve our effectiveness as we go through these cycles.

Deliberate learning is a skill that is developed through practice. The learning way is not a 24/7 life of learning. When we are immersed in a task, we may not be thinking about the model of how we should be going about the task. Thinking about the learning cycle may be most useful before we engage in learning and after we engage in action. We can use the cycle to plan strategies for engaging and mastering our immediate learning task or life situation. The concept of *flow,* where we become totally immersed in our work, is the opposite of deliberate learning, which emphasizes consciously evaluating feedback and making corrections in our actions. As we practice deliberate learning and build flexibility, our greater range of learning styles can allow us to respond to situations without breaking the flow of our work.

Start Small with One Big Thing

At the end of chapter four, you challenged yourself to identify a capability you want to acquire or a weakness you want to overcome. As you approach your flexibility goal, focus on small incremental steps using daily practice—be the tortoise instead of the hare: slow and steady wins the race. The key is not to try for big, sweeping changes all at once. Instead, create a series of new experiences on which you can reflect, think, and act that will move you in the general direction of your goal. In the same way that New Year's resolutions are rarely effective, setting a dramatic goal may be so overwhelming that it actually forces you back into your comfort zone.

Marion learned this when her new HR position required her to make presentations to employees. She resolved to overcome the paralysis she felt when she tried to speak publicly. This involved expanding her capabilities with the Initiating style. When she threw herself in front of a group of skeptics without adequate preparation, she set herself back; she could witness herself using a fixed mindset that told her she was not capable. Marion regrouped to apply what she had learned about learning. She began to plan small experiments that would allow her to practice little bits of the complex capabilities that are involved in making presentations.

First, she engaged in conversations with new acquaintances, which allowed her to practice thinking in the moment. Next, she tried giving short improvisational speeches to friends who offered feedback. Later, she focused on developing language and phrases that would resonate with her audiences. Marion also worked on her physical presence by breathing and grounding. With each new experience, she built her courage and began to think of herself as capable of thinking on her feet and connecting with her audience. After practicing over the course of months and years, one day Marion realized that she no longer felt nervous in front of large groups. Although it had happened slowly over time, she had transformed her ability to manage something that had once been out of her range. Using one brushstroke at a time, Marion completed an entire masterpiece. No longer did she avoid situations that called on the Initiating style. Marion could also use this situation to generalize her ability to build flexibility. When she realized that she did not possess capabilities in other learning styles, she thought, "I simply don't know how to do this *yet.*"

What about the time involved to make big changes? We all know that learning involves repeated practice, but the amount of time spent practicing is not necessarily a good predictor of performance. Going to the golf practice range and hitting bucket after bucket of balls doesn't necessarily improve your game and in fact may make it worse by ingraining bad habits.

Expert performance research initiated in the early 1990s by K. Anders Ericsson teaches us a great deal about learning from practice. The good news from this work is that greatness, for the most part, is not a function of innate talent; it is learned from experience. The not-so-good news is that greatness involves long-term commitment and hard work. To become a highly skilled expert can take an estimated 10,000 hours of deliberate practice or 20 hours a week for 50 weeks a year for ten years.[6] The basic techniques of deliberate practice are useful for improving our ability to deliberately learn from experience. Deliberate practice is like mindful experiencing with the addition of focused reflection on our concrete performance. When we reflect on our performance, we compare it against an ideal model to improve our future action in a recurring cycle of learning.

A key to successful learning is establishing the appropriate time frame expectation for achieving our learning goals. The most common error is the expectation created when setting goals of a "quick fix" and instant mastery. Perhaps one of the best examples of this is how, when we don't achieve immediate success with a diet, we abandon our dieting. To embark on a "lose ten pounds in ten days" diet is to limit ourselves to one turn through the learning cycle, while weight control is a long-term process with spirals of learning around many issues like calorie intake and exercise. Old habits are stubborn, and setbacks and failures are inevitable. The same is true about acquiring the capabilities of a new learning style. By framing the learning process correctly as one that will happen with slow progress over time, we can set ourselves up to stick with the process of building flexibility, not quit or view ourselves as having a fixed identity.

In *Mastery,* George Leonard describes the master's journey as a path that follows a recurring cycle of brief spurts of progress followed by dips of performance and a plateau of performance that is slightly higher than before where nothing seems to be happening until the next spurt. Many find this path, particularly the long plateaus, frustrating and abandon their efforts to learn and develop. Leonard writes, "You practice diligently, but you practice primarily *for the sake of practice itself.* Rather than being frustrated while on the plateau, you learn to appreciate and enjoy it as much as you do the upward surges."[7]

Leonard is confirming the importance of paying attention to the process rather than the outcome. Although it may seem paradoxical, when we focus on process rather than outcome, we open ourselves up to be more creative and relaxed, allowing us to actually perform better and enjoy the activity more. Therefore, if you stick with the process of learning all nine styles of learning, you will eventually experience flexibility in your learning style repertoire, although it may just happen in fits and starts.

When you trust the learning process, you avoid an excessive focus on the outcomes of immediate performance. You can focus instead on tracking your performance progress over time and from a distance. Rarely is a single performance test a matter of life and death, and to treat it as such only reinforces a fixed identity. Every performance is an occasion for learning and improvement in future performances.

Redefine Failure

One common roadblock to trying new behaviors and attitudes—even tiny ones—is the fear of failure. No one likes to fail, but failure is an inevitable part of doing something new. Thomas Edison, a role model for the learning way, said, "Failure is the most important ingredient for success."[8] In her commencement address to the 2008 graduates of Harvard University, J.K. Rowling described the low period in her life after graduation, which was marked by failure on every front, and talked about its benefits:

...failure meant a stripping away of the inessential. I stopped pretending to myself that I was anything other than what I was, and began to direct my energy into finishing the only work that mattered to me. Had I succeeded at anything else, I might never have found the determination to succeed in the one arena where I believed I truly belonged. I was set free because my greatest fear had been realized and I was still alive, and I still had a daughter whom I

adored, and I had an old typewriter and a big idea.
[9]

When you control your emotional responses to learn from failure, you empower yourself in an important way. When failures, losses, and mistakes provoke destructive emotional responses, they can block learning and feed into a fixed identity. The need for perfect performance and winning at any expense will block learning and keep you locked into familiar habits. Golfers who slam their club and curse themselves and the game after a bad shot lose the opportunity to coolly analyze their mistake and plan for corrections on the next round. In order to expand your learning flexibility, you will need to break out of your comfort zone and take some risks. Do this by focusing on the process instead of the outcome. Go in the general direction of your goal instead of having an all-or-nothing mentality. Is your learning flexibility high? Maybe *not yet,* but it is only because you have not practiced enough. It's only a matter of time and practice. Risk failure in the short term to maximize this opportunity.

Implementing the Learning Way

The learning way is an approach to living. It is a lifelong process that requires deep trust in your experiences along with a healthy skepticism about longstanding beliefs you might have about yourself and the world around you. You must embrace both quiet reflection and a passionate commitment to action in the face of uncertainty. You must remind yourself that growth involves risk and failure, but failure does not reflect on your ability to learn and grow.

Once you commit to learning and developing from your life experiences, you can begin to use the learning cycle to examine your learning style, your habits, your comfort zone, your relationships, your career, and your greater purpose. You can begin to see the benefits and drawbacks of each learning style, embrace different styles in different situations, and appreciate the diversity of preferred learning styles within your relationships at work and at home. Eventually you will be able to move through the learning cycle with ease, using each style in your own way to acquire new skills, make confident decisions, and gracefully adapt to changing situations.

How to Learn Anything Checklist for Action

As you tackle new challenges, make sure to return to the learning cycle, your learning style, and your learning flexibility profile to assess how you may have changed and how you might be able to take a different approach to continue developing new capabilities. You can use the Checklist for How to Learn Anything as a quick reference to guide you through the lifelong process of learning. Use this checklist to remember to use all the learning styles for deliberate learning:

- **Experiencing:** Use mindfulness, intentional attention, and focusing to tune into your feelings and physical sensations and empathize with others. What problem are you facing? What is happening now?

- **Imagining:** Brainstorm different responses to your experiences. What are the possibilities concerning your feeling and sensations? What can you learn from the experiences of others? What are some possibilities for an ideal outcome?

- **Reflecting:** Connect your sensations with general ideas to make sense of them. Seek the perspectives of other people you trust and admire. Have your experiences revealed new aspects of your situation? Do you have any new questions you need to ask before moving forward?

- **Analyzing:** Compile all of the information that you will need to make a decision and organize it. Use this information to create a plan. Do you have all the information needed to make a decision?

- **Thinking:** Connect the information you analyzed to broader information you have. How does your experience fit in with your previous experiences or the experiences of people you know? Should you take any of that information into account? Are there any related subjects you could investigate to help you make a decision?

- **Deciding:** Set a goal—start small—and figure out the first step you can take toward reaching that goal. Determine how you will measure your progress as you move toward your goal. Do you need to build in reminders to check in with yourself or with other people to keep you accountable?

- **Acting:** Begin executing your plan, starting with the first step you decided on. Are you able to implement your plan with existing resources?

- **Initiating:** Seek out new opportunities for implementing your plan, building new capabilities, refining your approach, and engaging others. What new experiences could you seek out to help you continue to grow? What do you need to alter as you try again?

- **Balancing:** Ask yourself whether your approach is working as well as it could be. Should you consider shifting to a new learning style to accomplish your task? As you work toward accomplishing your goals, make sure to make time to practice mindfulness and return to your experience. With that, the cycle begins again in a lifelong process of learning and growth.

Practice Learning Anything

- Develop a long-term plan. Look for improvements and payoffs over months and years, rather than right away.

- Look for safe ways to practice new skills. Find situations that test them, and don't punish yourself if you fail. Take time to consciously learn from your mistakes.

- Return to your learning flexibility profile regularly. Each time you face a new learning situation or take on a new project, use the full learning cycle to anticipate different approaches you can take that will help you develop new learning skills.

- Reward yourself—becoming a flexible learner is hard work.

- Align learning with your core values. When your efforts satisfy meaningful values, you are optimally motivated to keep learning, growing, gaining wisdom, and building competence.

Reflect on Learning Anything

You may find it helpful to journal about your use of learning flexibility in your current life situation. Below you will find prompts for your reflections.

- We develop and grow as human beings through learning, and this process continues long after we finish our formal education. Think of a time after you were out of school when you learned something about yourself or the world. How did you integrate that new knowledge into your life? Did it change how you think of yourself?

- Think of a major life transition that you went through. How did you decide to deal with that challenge? Now that you are aware of the learning cycle, can you think of a different way that you could have made your transition?

- What potential challenges or transitions can you foresee on the horizon? Apply the learning cycle to reflect on how you might respond to future challenges as opportunities for personal growth.

- Think about how you felt when reading about the learning way approach to life. Did you start thinking of how you could address a current challenge in your life or learn a new skill? Make a list of goals that you would like to work toward using the learning cycle. As you work toward these goals and build your capacity to learn deliberately, monitor your progress and pay attention to your learning process in real time. This will help you live by the process of learning and transform your life.

Notes

Introduction

[1]   Arbaugh, J.B., Dearmond, S., and Rau, B.L., "New Uses for Existing Tools? A Call to Study Online Management Instruction and Instructors," *AMLE,* vol.12, no.4, 2013, pp.635–655.

Chapter One: The Learning Way

[1]   Oprah Winfrey, BrainyQuote.com., September 10, `2016, www.brainyquote.com/quotes/quotes /o/oprahwinfr133519.html.

[2]   Kahneman, Daniel, and Jason Riis, "Living and Thinking about It: Two Perspectives on Life," *The Science of Well-Being,* edited by N. Baylis, Felicia A. Huppert, and B. Keverne, Oxford University Press, 2005 pp.285–301.

[3]   Rogers, Carl, "Toward a Modern Approach to Values: The Valuing Process in the Mature Person," *Journal of Abnormal and Social Psychology,* vol 63, no.2, 1964, pp.160–167.

[4]   Maturana, H.R. and Varela, F., *Autopoeisis and Cognition.* Reidel, 1980.

[5]   Maslow, Abraham H., *Toward a Psychology of Being.* Second Edition, Van Nostrand Reinhold, 1968.

[6]   Rogers, Carl, "Toward a Modern Approach to Values: The Valuing Process in the Mature Person." *Journal of Abnormal and Social Psychology,* vol.63, no.2, 1964, pp.160–167.

[7]   Dewey, John, *Democracy and Education.* Macmillan Company, 1916.

Chapter Two: I Am a Learner

[1]   Dweck, Carol S., *Self-Theories: Their Role in Motivation, Personality, and Development,* Psychology Press, Taylor & Francis Group, 2000.

[2]   Zull, James, *From Brain to Mind: Using Neuroscience to Guide Change in Education,* Stylus, 2011.

[3]   Bargh, J.A. and Chartrand, T.L., "The Unbearable Automaticity of Being," *American Psychologist,* vol 54, no.7, 1999, pp.462–479.

[4]   Freire, Paulo, *Pedagogy of the Oppressed,* The Seabury Press, 1970.

[5]   Zull, James, *The Art of Changing the Brain,* Stylus, 2002, pp.18–19.

Chapter 3: My Learning Style, My Life Path

[1]   Horton, Miles and Freire, Paulo, *We Make the Road by Walking,* Temple University Press, 1990.

Chapter Four: Building Learning Style Flexibility

[1]   Sharma, Garima and Kolb, David A., "The Learning Flexibility Index: Assessing Contextual Flexibility in Learning Style," in S. Rayner and E. Cools (Eds.), *Style Differences in Cognition, Learning and Management: Theory, Research and Practice,* Routledge, 2010, pp.60–77.

[2]   Kolb, David A. and Wolfe Donald, with collaborators, "Professional Education and Career Development: A Cross-Sectional Study of Adaptive Competencies in Experiential Learning," final report NIE grant no. NIE-G-77-0053, 1981. ERIC no. ED 209493CE 030 519. This study is described in Kolb, David A., *Experiential Learning: Experience as the Source of Learning and Development,* Prentice-Hall, 1984, pp.184–196.

Chapter Five: Learning Flexibility and the Road Ahead

[1]   Bridges William, *Managing Transitions: Making the Most of Change,* Da Capo Lifelong Books, 2009.

[2]   Dane, Erik, "Reconsidering the Trade-Off between Expertise and Flexibility: A Cognitive Entrenchment Perspective," *The Academy of Management Review,* vol.35, no.4, October 2010, pp.579-603.

[3]   Freire, Paulo, *Pedagogy of the Oppressed,* The Seabury Press, 1970.

Chapter Six: What's Next? Deliberate Learning for Life

[1]   Dewey, John, *How We Think: A Restatement of the Relation of Reflective Thinking to the Educative Process,* D.C. Heath and Company, 1933.

[2]   Kabat-Zinn, J., *Wherever You Go, There You Are,* Hyperion, 1994, p.4.

[3]   Rogers, Carl, *On Becoming a Person,* Houghton Mifflin, 1961, pp.151–52.

[4]   Gendlin, Eugene T., *Focusing,* Bantam Books, 1978, p.127

[5]   Gendlin, Eugene T., *Focusing,* Bantam Books, 1978, pp.127–128.

[6]   Ericsson, K. Anders and Charness, N., "Expert Performance: Its Structure and Acquisition," *American Psychologist,* vol.49, no.8, 1994, p.725.

[7]   Leonard, G., *Mastery: The Keys to Success and Long-Term Fulfillment.* Penguin Group, 1992, p.17.

[8]   London, Manuel,*The Oxford Handbook of Lifelong Learning,* New York: Oxford University Press, 2011, p.83

[9]   Rowling, J.K., "A Stripping Away of the Inessential," *Harvard Magazine,* July-August 2008, pp.55–56.

References

Experiential Learning Theory is a synthesis of the works those great scholars who gave experience a central role in their theories of human learning and development. We have come to call them the "foundational scholars of experiential learning": William James, John Dewey, Kurt Lewin, Jean Piaget, Lev Vygotsky, Carl Jung, Mary Parker Follett, Carl Rogers, and Paulo Freire. The figure below depicts these foundational scholars of ELT and a summary of their contributions to experiential learning. Their contributions span over one hundred years beginning the end of the nineteenth century with William James, John Dewey, and Mary Parker Follett and ending at the end of the twentieth century with the deaths of Carl Rogers and Paulo Freire.

Arbaugh, J.B., Dearmond, S and Rau, B.L. "New Uses for Existing Tools? A Call to Study Online Management Instruction and Instructors." *AMI F,* vol.12, no.4, 2013, pp.635–655.

Bargh, J.A., and Chartrand, T.L. "The Unbearable Automaticity of Being." *American Psychologist,* vol.54, no.7, 1999, pp.462–479.

Bateson, Gregory. *Steps to an Ecology of Mind: Collected Essays in Anthropology, Psychiatry, Evolution and Epistemology.* Northvale, NJ: Jason Aronson, Inc., 1972.

Baxter-Magolda, M.B. "Self-Authorship: The Foundation for Twenty-First Century Education." *New Directions for Teaching and Learning* 109, 2007, 69–83.

Baxter-Magolda, M.B. "Three Elements of Self-Authorship." *Journal of College Student Development,* vol.49, no.4, 2008, 269–284.

Boyatzis, R.E., and Kolb, D.A. "Performance, Learning and Development as Modes of Growth and Adaptation throughout Our Lives and Careers." In M. Peiperl et al. (Eds.), *Career Frontiers: New Conceptions of Working Lives.* London: Oxford University Press, 1999.

Boyatzis, Richard E. and Kolb, David A. "Assessing Individuality in Learning: The Learning Skills Profile." *Educational Psychology,* vol.11, nos 3 and 4, 1991.

Bridges, William. *Managing Transitions: Making the Most of Change.* Boston, MA: Da Capo Lifelong Books, 2009.

Brinol, P., and Petty, R.E. "Overt Head Movements and Persuasion: A Self-Validation Analysis." *Journal of Personality and Social Psychology,* vol.84, 2003, 1123–1139.

Brown, K.W., and Ryan, R.M., "The Benefits of Being Present: Mindfulness and Its Role in Psychological Well-Being," *Journal of Personality and Social Psychology,* vol.84, 2003, pp.822–848.

Carney, Dana R., Cuddy, Amy J.C., and Yap, Andy J. "Power Posing: Brief Nonverbal Displays Affect

Neuroendocrine Levels and Risk Tolerance." *Psychological Science,* vol.21, 2010, pp.1363–1368.

Clay, T.A. *What Are the Obligations of Partners?* Newtown Square, PA: Altman Weil, Inc., 2002.

Dane, Erik. "Reconsidering the Trade-Off between Expertise and Flexibility: A Cognitive Entrenchment Perspective." *The Academy of Management Review,* vol.35, no.4, 2010, pp.599–603.

Dewey, J. *Democracy and Education.* New York: Macmillan Company, 1916.

Dewey, John. *How We Think: A Restatement of the Relation of Reflective Thinking to the Educative Process.* New York: D.C. Heath and Company, 1933.

Dweck, C.S. "Motivational Processes Affecting Learning." *American Psychologist,* vol.41, no.10, 1986, pp.1040–1048.

Dweck, C.S. *Self-Theories: Their Role in Motivation, Personality, and Development.* Psychology Press. Florence, KY: Taylor & Francis Group, 2000.

Ericcson, K.A. and Charness, L. "Expert Performance: Its Structure and Acquisition," *American Psychologist,* 49(8), 1994, 725–747.

Ericsson K.A., Krampe, R.T., and Tesch-Römer, C. "The Role of Deliberate Practice in the Acquisition of Expert Performance," *Psychological Review* vol.100, 1993, pp.363–406.

Ericsson, K.A. and Charness, N. "Expert Performance: Its Structure and Acquisition." *American Psychologist,* vol.49, no.8, 2010, p.725.

Fredrickson, B.L. *Positivity: Groundbreaking Research Reveals How to Embrace the Hidden Strength of Positive Emotions, Overcome Negativity, and Thrive.* New York: Crown Publishing, 2009.

Freire, Paulo. *Pedagogy of the Oppressed.* New York: The Seabury Press, 1970.

Gallagher, W. *Rapt: Attention and the Focused Life.* New York: Penguin Group, 2009.

Gendlin, Eugene T. *Focusing.* New York: Bantam Books, 1978.

Hackney, Peggy. *Making Connections: Total Body Integration through Bartenieff Fundamentals.* New York: Routledge, 2002.

Hall, N. *The Making of Higher Executives: The Modern Challenges.* New York University, 1958.

Hofsteade, G. *Culture's Consequences: International Differences in Work Related Values.* Beverly Hills, CA: Sage Publications, 1980.

Horton, Miles and Freire, Paulo. *We Make the Road by Walking.* Philadelphia: Temple University Press, 1990.

Johnson, B. *Polarity Management: Identifying and Managing Unsolvable Problems.* Amherst, MA: HRD Press, Inc., 2014.

Joiner, B. and Josephs, S. *Leadership Agility: Five Levels of Mastery for Anticipating and Initiating Change.* San Francisco: Jossey-Bass, 2007.

Jostmann, N.B., Lakens, D., and Schubert, T.W. "Weight as an Embodiment of Importance." *Psychological Science,* vol.20, 2009, pp.1169–1174.

Kabat-Zinn, J. *Wherever You Go, There You Are.* New York: Hyperion, 1994.

Kahneman, D. *Thinking, Fast and Slow.* New York: Farrar, Straus and Giroux, 2011.

Kegan, Robert. *In Over Our Heads: The Demands of Modern Life.* Cambridge, MA: Harvard University Press, 1994.

Kolb, Alice Y., and Kolb, David A. (2005). "Learning Styles and Learning Spaces: Enhancing Experiential Learning in Higher Education." *Academy of Management Learning & Education,* vol.4, 2005, pp.193–212.

Kolb, Alice. Y. and Kolb, David A. *Experiential Learning Theory Bibliography: Volume 1–5 1971–2016.* Cleveland, OH: Experience Based Learning Systems, Inc., 2016. www.learningfromexperience.com

Kolb, Alice Y. and Kolb, David A. Research Library Experiential Learning. http://learningfromexperience.com/research/

Kolb, David A. *Experiential Learning: Experience as the Source of Learning and Development.* 2nd edition. Upper Saddle River, NJ: Pearson Education, 2015.

Kolb, David A. "Learning Styles and Disciplinary Differences: Diverse Pathways." In A. Chickering (ed.), *The Modern American College.* Jossey-Bass, 1981.

Kolb, David A. and Peterson, Kay. "Tailor Your Coaching to People's Learning Styles." *HBR Guide to Coaching Employees.* Boston, MA: Harvard Business Press Books, 2013.

Kolb, David A., and Donald Wolfe, with collaborators. "Professional Education and Career Development: A Cross-Sectional Study of Adaptive Competencies in Experiential Learning," final report NIE grant no. NIE-G-77-0053, 1981. ERIC no. ED 209493CE 030 519.

Lawler, E.E. and Worley, C.G. *Built to Change: How to Achieve Sustained Organizational Effectiveness.* San Francisco: Jossey-Bass, 2006.

Leonard, G. *Mastery: The Keys to Success and Long-Term Fulfillment.* New York: Penguin Group, 1992.

Leonard, G. *Mastery: The Keys to Long-Term Success and Fulfillment.* New York: Dutton, 1991.

Maddi, S.R. and Kobasa, S.C. *The Hardy Executive: Health under Stress.* Homewood, IL: Dow Jones-Irwin, 1984.

Maslow, Abraham H. *Toward a Psychology of Being.* Second edition. New York: Van Nostrand Reinhold, 1968.

Maturana, H. and Varela, F. *Autopoeisis and Cognition.* Dordrecht, Holland: D. Reidel, 1980.

Maturana, H. and Varela, F. *The Tree of Knowledge: Biological Roots of Human Understanding.* Boston: Shambala, 1987.

Miller, J.B. and Stiver, I. *The Healing Connection.* Boston: Beacon Press, 1997.

Pauchant, Thierry C. *In Search of Meaning: Managing for the Health of Our Organizations, Our Communities, and the Natural World.* San Francisco: Jossey-Bass, Inc., 1995.

Peterson, Kay, DeCato, Lisa, and Kolb, David A. "Moving and Learning: Expanding Style and Increasing Flexibility." *Journal of Experiential Education,* vol.38, no.3, 2015, pp.228–244.

Pfeffer, J. and Sutton, R.I. *The Knowing-Doing Gap: How Smart Companies Turn Knowledge into Action.* Boston: Harvard Business School Press, 2000.

Rogers, Carl. *On Becoming a Person.* Boston: Houghton Mifflin, 1961.

Rogers, Carl. "Toward a Modern Approach to Values: The Valuing Process in the Mature Person." *Journal of Abnormal and Social Psychology,* vol.63, no.2, 1964, pp.160–167.

Sharma, G. and Kolb, D.A. "The Learning Flexibility Index: Assessing Contextual Flexibility in Learning Style." In S. Rayner and E. Cools (Eds.), *Style Differences in Cognition, Learning, and Management: Theory, Research and Practice.* New York: Routledge, 2010, pp.60–77.

Sutcliffe, Kathleen M., Vogus, Timothy J., and Dane, Erik. "Mindfulness in Organizations: A Cross-Level Review." *Annual Review of Organizational Psychology and Organizational Behavior,* vol.3, 2016, pp.55–81.

Vaill, Peter B. *Learning as a Way of Being: Strategies for Survival in a World of Permanent White Water.* San Francisco: Jossey-Bass, 1996.

Wilcoxson, L. and Prosser, M. "Kolb's Learning Style Inventory (1985): Review and Further Study of Validity and Reliability." *British Journal of Educational Psychology,* vol.66, no.2, 1996, pp.247–257.

Winfrey, Oprah. BrainyQuote.com. Retrieved September 10, 2016.

Wolfe, D.M. and Kolb, D.A. "Beyond Specialization: The Quest for Integration in Mid-Career." In Brooklyn Derr (ed.), *Work, Family and the Career: New Frontiers in Theory and Research.* New York: Praeger Publishers, 1980, pp.239–281.

Zull, James. *From Brain to Mind: Using Neuroscience to Guide Change in Education.* Sterling, VA: Stylus, 2011.

Zull, James. *The Art of Changing the Brain.* Sterling, VA: Stylus, 2002.

Appendix A

The Kolb Learning Style Inventory 4.0

The Kolb Learning Style Inventory 4.0 (KLSI 4) was created to help you understand your unique way of learning and to use the insights gained to improve your learning power. The KLSI 4.0 describes the way you learn and how you deal with ideas and day-to-day situations. We all learn in different ways. This inventory can serve as a stimulus for you to interpret and reflect on the ways you prefer to learn in specific settings. Learning can be described as a cycle made up of four basic processes. The KLSI 4.0 takes you through those processes to give you better understanding of how you learn.

The KLSI 4.0 is the first major revision of the KLSI since 1999 and the third since the original LSI was published in 1971. Based on many years of research involving scholars around the world and data from many thousands of respondents, the KLSI 4.0 includes an assessment of the nine ways of learning and your personal learning style preference. The nine learning styles are Initiating, Experiencing, Imagining, Reflecting, Analyzing, Thinking, Deciding, Acting, and Balancing.

It also includes an assessment of learning flexibility. The nine learning styles are not fixed traits but dynamic states that can flex to meet the demands of different learning situations. For the first time the KLSI 4.0 includes a personal assessment of the degree to which a person changes their style in different learning contexts. The flexibility score also shows which ways of learning you use as a backup to your dominant learning style. This information can help you improve your ability to move freely around the learning cycle and improve your learning effectiveness in all areas of life.

You can take the KLSI 4.0 by going to www.learning fromexperience.com and clicking on the Learning Style Inventory Version Four under Featured Assessment Instruments. After taking the KLSI 4.0 online you will immediately be sent a personal report of your results. The personal report describes your learning strengths and will lead you through a process of applying them in your everyday life. In this report you will learn about:

- The cycle of learning from experience.

- Your learning style; the unique way you use the learning cycle to learn.

- The ways in which you prefer to learn, and how to use your preferences to maximize your learning.

- Your learning flexibility; your ability to fully use the learning cycle and modify your approach based on what you are learning about.

- How to strengthen and develop your learning style.

- How to apply what you have learned about yourself in your life: in your approach to problem-solving and decision making, dealing with conflict and disagreements, teamwork, communicating at work and at home, and your career development.

One person's KLSI 4 report results are shown on the next two pages.

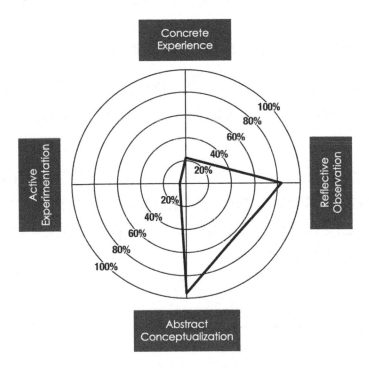

174

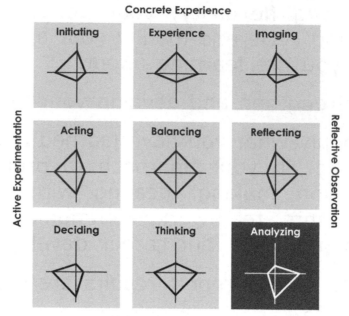

Your learning flexibility score

Your learning flexibility score is calculated by how much your learning style varies from situation to situation.

Your learning flexibility score is .59 which indicates that you show some flexibility; adapting your learning style to different situations but perhaps not using all four learning phases.

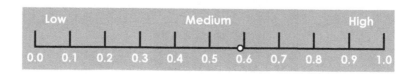

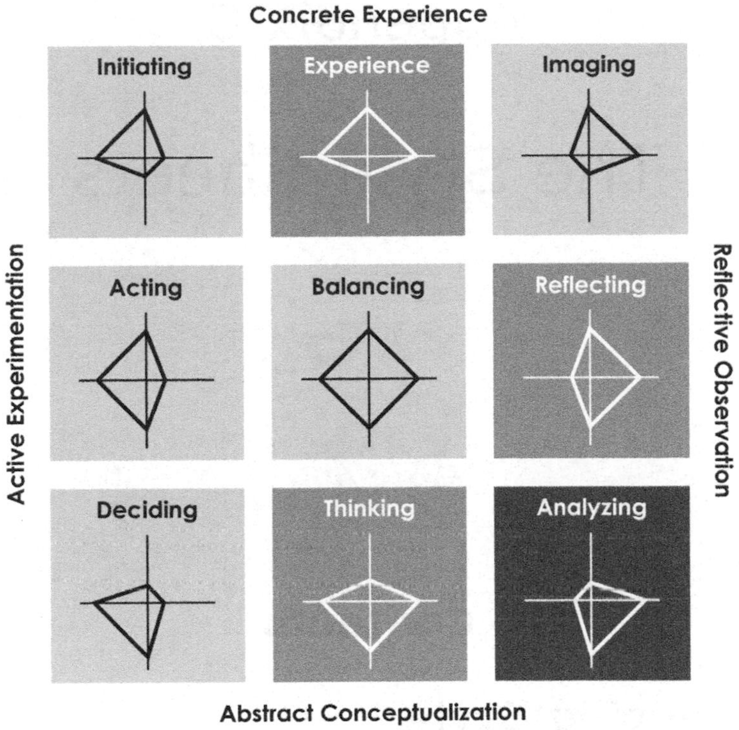
Concrete Experience
Initiating
Experience
Imaging
Acting
Balancing
Reflecting
Deciding
Thinking
Analyzing
Active Experimentation
Reflective Observation
Abstract Conceptualization

Appendix B

The Style Sheets

Contents

The Experiencing Style
The Imagining Style
The Reflecting Style
The Analyzing Style
The Thinking Style
The Deciding Style
The Acting Style
The Initiating Style
The Balancing Style

In this section, you will find a detailed profile of each learning style. Each profile features a general description of people who prefer that style, including their preferred environment, stressors, and capabilities; the drawbacks of overusing that style; tips for using the style to communicate and lead teams; and finally, tips for shifting into the style when it is unfamiliar to you.

Experiencing

Capabilities

Establishing trusting relationships
Being involved and engaged
Connecting personally when communicating
Being comfortable with emotional expression

Preferred Environments

Lively conversational spaces
Natural settings
Environments rich in sensory stimuli

Stressors

Making decisions without concern for the people
involved
Focusing on future plans without regard to the present
moment
Relying on facts alone
Being locked into a routine

Key Questions

Am I present to "what is"?
Am I grounded and aware of my breath?
Am I aware of my physical reaction?
What is my felt sense?
What is my intuition telling me?
Am I paying attention to my surroundings?
Do I trust my own experience to transform me in the moment?
Am I sensitive to others and to myself?

"Happiness, not in another place but this place ... not for another hour, but this hour."

—*Walt Whitman*

Description: Your Inner Connector

If you prefer the Experiencing style, you are adept at connecting with others in deep relationships. You are insightful, empathetic, warm, and engaging. Expressing your emotions probably is comfortable for you. You know how to be present and engaged in whatever is happening around you. This mindfulness extends to your awareness of your five senses. You relish being able to touch, see, hear, taste, and smell. Dining with friends, making a delicious meal, feeling different textures, and spending time in nature may be some of your favorite activities.

You may prefer to approach your personal development through having rich conversations with others, practicing mindfulness, and paying attention to what you can learn from your emotions and physical sensations.

Overusing the Experiencing Style

If you overuse the Experiencing style, you probably dread the word "objectivity." You may become overly emotional or call exclusively on your inner circle of friends rather than seeking out critical evaluation. Overusing the Experiencing style may cause others to lose trust in you because your decisions are not always grounded in logic.

Using the Experiencing Style to Lead a Team

The strength of the experiencing style is a focus on relationships and the big picture. Build team spirit to make connections and promote team members' confidence to express new ideas. When you are leading a group process, remain self-aware and identify your feelings and intuition as well as the feelings of your team. Be open to new information that sparks unconventional approaches and innovation. As your team members progress in their work, use stories and drama to engage them emotionally. Inspire, build relationships, and help team members succeed.

Communicating in the Experiencing Style

When you want to communicate in the Experiencing style or communicate with someone who prefers the Experiencing style, begin by focusing on your emotions and feelings. This helps you connect with others on a personal level. Strive to remain open, listen, and accept. Then work toward using language that is sensitive and engages emotions, incorporating stories, metaphors, and creative writing into your communication. Address conflict in a warm, personalized way, and defuse tension by acknowledging emotions and the shared desire to feel good when the conflict is resolved.

Key Phrases

"Something feels off to me."

"How is everyone feeling?"

Here is a typical e-mail communication using the Experiencing style:

Subject: Meeting tomorrow

Message: Please join us tomorrow at noon. We will be meeting in the conference room for lunch prior to the start of our formal agenda so that we can get to know our new

182

team members. Looking forward to being together.

Flexing to the Experiencing Style

In the Experiencing style, you can learn to connect with others and with yourself: your emotions, your physical sensations, and your intuition. You become able to engage with whatever situation you face instead of becoming detached and dispassionate. Rather than reliving the past or worrying about the future, you learn to become present in the moment and aware of what you are experiencing with your five senses. This awareness helps you tune in to concrete experiences—that is, specific situations instead of general concepts. You can use this awareness as a foundation for your decisions.

You should flex to the Experiencing style when you want to recognize your emotions and physical sensations; connect, communicate, and collaborate with others; and be present and mindful in your environments. To begin flexing to the Experiencing style, you can embody the physical characteristics of the style, practice exercises that draw your attention to the capabilities of the style, or ask yourself key questions that will help remind you how to use the style effectively.

Use your body to help you flex to the Experiencing style:

Place your sensory perceptions on high alert.

Turn your attention to your sensations, your emotions, and your environment.

Use a wide field of vision to take in a broad view of a situation.

Use these techniques to begin flexing to the Experiencing style:

Focus on your breathing.

Take a walk in nature.

Develop awareness of your senses.

Imagining

Capabilities

Generating new ideas
Demonstrating empathy for others
Seeking others' opinions
Imagining new possibilities

Preferred Environments

Lively conversational spaces
Natural settings
Environments rich in sensory stimuli

Stressors

Focusing on one "right" path
Focusing on details needed to complete projects
Lacking harmony in relationships
Excluding people or ideas

Key Questions

Am I promoting trust?
Do I have unconditional positive regard?
Have I included everyone?
Am I receptive to all possibilities?
Do I have diverse sources of information?
Can I find more?
Have I judged too soon?
Am I listening with an open mind?
What can I do to help?

"The very essence of the creative is its novelty, and hence we have no standard by which to judge it."

—Carl Rogers

Description: Your Inner Dreamer

If you prefer the Imagining style, you are sensitive to the feelings of others, and you demonstrate this empathy through your ability to listen. You recognize patterns—in events, relationships, and interactions—and make meaning from them. You are more comfortable leaving things open than narrowing down the options before it is necessary.

You may prefer to approach your personal development with creativity. You might even think of your own self-development as a creative project.

Overusing the Imagining Style

If you overuse the Imagining style, you probably dread the word "choose." You may be indiscriminate or undervalue the practical results of reaching a goal. You may find yourself losing focus when working toward a goal, reopening discussions that have resulted in decisions, focusing on others more than on yourself and allowing your empathy to prevent you from making decisions, or feeling disorganized or unable to complete projects.

Using the Imagining Style to Lead a Team

The strength of the Imagining style is creating a culture that is open to new ideas and new people. When you are leading a group process, recruit people who value and believe in you, and allow for conversation and debate. As your team members progress in their work, slow down decisions that are being made prematurely and minimize interpersonal upset and drama by acknowledging your team members' feelings and coaching them to resolve differences. Value different opinions and ideas as a source of information, and be open to new information that sparks unconventional approaches and innovation.

Communicating in the Imagining Style

When you want to communicate in the Imagining style or communicate with someone who prefers the Imagining style, begin by asking powerful questions that encourage new ideas. Brainstorm, reach for the stars, and create an ideal vision. Use words that convey empathy and trust, listen closely to what people have to say, and strive to include everyone in a conversation while taking a pulse on each person's feelings. Create alternative paths to a situation that unite and inspire others. Address conflict after making a personal connection based on shared values, and defuse tension by showing a warm, easygoing approach, expressing the intent to maintain a positive connection, and being empathetic.

Key Phrases

"How can I help?"

"Let's imagine the possibilities."

"What other information do we need?"

Here is a typical e-mail communication using the Imagining style:

Subject: Tomorrow's meeting

Message: Please come to tomorrow's meeting with all of your new ideas for the program. We want this to be a great experience for the entire team. Is there anyone else who should be included who has not been cc'd on this e-mail? Thanks.

Flexing to the Imagining Style

In the Imagining style, you can learn to gather information from diverse sources, generate ideas, and create a vision. You can begin to seek novelty, envision possibilities, and connect with your values. Rather than dwell on details, you learn to see the big picture. This awareness helps you consider new, diverse approaches to solving problems.

You should flex to the Imagining style when you want to demonstrate empathy, appreciate diversity, and expand your horizons. To begin flexing to the Imagining style, you can embody the physical characteristics of the style, practice exercises that draw your attention to the capabilities of the style, or ask yourself key questions that will help remind you how to use the style effectively.

Use your body to help you flex to the Imagining style:

Be relaxed and adopt a leisurely pace.

Imagine yourself becoming lighter, more open, and gentle.

Use warm, inviting movements to draw people in.

Use these techniques to begin flexing to the Imagining style:

Imagine three possible solutions for any one problem.

Place yourself in new cultural settings with an attitude of curiosity and no goal in mind.

When speaking with someone, ask three questions before making a judgment.

Reflecting

Capabilities

Listening with an open mind
Gathering information from a variety of sources
Identifying underlying problems and issues
Viewing issues from many perspectives

Preferred Environments

Natural, solitary settings
Spaces that inspire journaling with rich visual imagery
 and auditory stimuli
Environments that allow for contemplation, creation,
 and discovery
Quiet spaces for pursuing independent projects

Stressors

Feeling the urgency to act
Making mistakes
Taking a public stand without preparation

Key Questions

Have I considered thought-provoking questions?
Am I allowing time to struggle and find answers?
Can I slow things down?
Have I considered other points of view?
Have I observed and deliberated?
Have I taken time to recuperate?

"Life can only be understood backwards; but it must be lived forwards."

—Soren Kierkegaard

Description: Your Inner Observer

If you prefer the Reflecting style, you probably dread the word "now." You connect experience and ideas through sustained contemplation. You dive into thoughts and observations and mull over information from every perspective. You find the deeper meaning that underlies the obvious. Because you are a great observer and understand so much, you find it easy to be sensitive to the feelings and needs of others. You may be quiet in groups, but there is always something insightful going on inside that head of yours. Given the opportunity, you love to have deep conversations to continue the sense-making process. You just have to take your time.

You may prefer to approach your personal development with rehearsing, visualization, and careful thought.

Overusing the Reflecting Style

If you overuse the Reflecting style, you may have trouble implementing goals or taking action. This can cause you to miss opportunities. You may also have trouble keeping track of time and maintaining your energy or sense of urgency throughout a project.

Using the Reflecting Style to Lead a Team

The strength of the Reflecting style is recognizing the connection between feelings and thoughts. When you are leading a group process, create effective processes that incorporate the needs of people and the need for accurate information, inquiry, and advocacy. As your team members progress in their work, slow down decisions that arc being made prematurely.

Communicating in the Reflecting Style

When you want to communicate in the Reflecting style or communicate with someone who prefers the Reflecting style, begin slowly and thoughtfully by asking powerful questions to go deeper. Listen carefully and build credibility by weighing your words and ideas prior to speaking. Take time, be cautious, pause, process ideas, and observe role models. Address conflict slowly, asking questions along the way. Defuse tension by being patient and allowing for time alone before making decisions.

Key Phrases

"Let me explore this further."

"Can I get back to you after I have time to think this through?"

(Sometimes, simply be silent.)

Here is a typical e-mail communication using the Reflecting style:

Subject: Tomorrow's Meeting

Message: During our meeting tomorrow, please be prepared to offer your perspective on the proposed policy. We want to have time to hear every angle and make sense of unintended consequences before we decide if we should adopt it.

Flexing to the Reflecting Style

In the Reflecting style, you are able to consider multiple perspectives by listening and observing. You can exercise patience to be thorough. Rather than jump to a decision or conclusion, you learn to become interested in the process. This awareness of the process can help you make people and things work effectively to minimize downsides.

You should flex to the Reflecting style when you want to recuperate, make sense of feelings and thoughts, listen with an open mind, or consider the best action to take while remaining calm in urgent or ambiguous situations. To begin flexing to the Reflecting style, you can embody the physical characteristics of the style, practice exercises that draw your attention to the capabilities of the style, or ask yourself key questions that will help remind you of how to use the style effectively.

Use your body to help you flex to the Reflecting style:

Remain still and calm.

Be deliberate and unhurried in your movements.

Use these techniques to begin flexing to the Reflecting style:

Try debating a topic from one side of the argument, then from the other side. Notice what happens to your perspective when you assume these positions.

Repeat and rephrase statements directed at you, especially those that are emotionally charged, for clarity and understanding.

Take a new route home and notice ten different things.

Analyzing

Capabilities

Planning ahead to minimize mistakes
Organizing information to get the full picture
Analyzing data
Using theories and models to explain

Preferred Environments

Quiet environments with few distractions
Solitary spaces that allow for detailed work

Stressors

Feeling a sense of urgency
Being in unstable, chaotic environments
Needing to constantly be in communication
Participating in large groups in an intimidating
 atmosphere

Key Questions

Have I been thorough and precise?
Can I use a model or theory to explain?
Can I provide data or specialized knowledge?
Are my thoughts organized?
Have I considered the best structure?
Have I eliminated distractions?

"There is nothing so practical as a good theory."

—*Kurt Lewin*

Description: Your Inner Planner

If you prefer the Analyzing style, you like to organize and systematize vast quantities of information. Your ideal way of learning is to plan ahead to minimize mistakes by taking a structured, methodical approach. To do this, you use your skills of control, restraint, and organization. In the Analyzing style, you adopt an objective stance with no emotional interference. You tend to be more comfortable in controllable research conditions than in messy relationships.

You may prefer to approach your personal development with careful planning in settings that allow for some control and management.

Overusing the Analyzing Style

If you overuse the Analyzing style, you probably dread the word "improvise." You may become fixated on the details of a project without making progress toward a goal. Your rigid need for structure may cause you to be critical and exacting, and you may feel the need to control all variables. You may find yourself avoiding people to work alone.

Using the Analyzing Style to Lead a Team

The strength of the Analyzing style is providing facts and logic before taking action. When you are leading a group process, maintain clarity of purpose to help your team members understand why their work is important. As your team members progress in their work, use your analytical skills to manage projects with precision. Help your team members stay on task by setting objectives based on a strategic plan.

Communicating in the Analyzing Style

When you want to communicate in the Analyzing style or communicate with someone who prefers the Analyzing style, begin by using concise, logical language—seek details, organize facts, synthesize data, use research, and create a plan. Use theories or conceptual models to test your assumptions and ideas before applying them. Address conflict by focusing on facts and showing appreciation for the contribution of the other people in the situation. Defuse tension by acknowledging your collaborators' expertise, respecting their unique approach, and avoiding the urge to become emotional.

Key Phrases

"Let's get organized."

"I've created a graphic to illustrate this point."

"How can we minimize mistakes?"

Here is a typical e-mail communication using the Analyzing style:

Subject: Tomorrow's meeting

Message: Tomorrow we will be meeting to discuss our approach to providing service to our new client. It took us 6.8 months to capture the business—130 percent over our average, so we want to make sure to carefully plan our strategy. We anticipate that this new work will add 23 percent to our gross revenue this calendar year. Attached, please find a graph that details the income breakdown by division. Let me know if you have any questions.

Flexing to the Analyzing Style

In the Analyzing style, you can learn to carefully approach the details of a situation. You become able to organize and synthesize abundant information into a logical form. This ability can help you develop concise theories about what the information might mean and how you should respond to it.

You should flex to the Analyzing style when you want to organize and synthesize detailed data, develop models and theories to explain information, remain unemotional and analytical, or be accurate and precise. To begin flexing to the Analyzing style, you can embody the physical characteristics of the style, practice exercises that draw your attention to the capabilities of the style, or ask yourself key questions that will help remind you of how to use the style effectively.

Use your body to help you flex to the Analyzing style:

> Be closed, narrow and rounded, as if you are sitting at a computer.

> Focus your mind and hold yourself still for long periods.

> Use precise, controlled movements.

Use these techniques to begin flexing to the Analyzing style:

Create a budget that includes every detail of your spending plan.

Study a theory or model; for instance, take time to understand the learning cycle and your own learning preferences.

Learn how to use a new feature on your smart phone or computer.

Thinking

Capabilities

Using data to analyze solutions
Framing arguments with logic
Using critical thinking for objective communication
Making independent judgments

Preferred Environments

Predictable, controllable environments
Spaces that allow for time alone without distractions

Stressors

Being in emotional situations
Facing unclear expectations
Working with others without time alone
Being in chaotic environments

Key Questions

Am I focused?
Am I aware of my thoughts?
What is my logic telling me?
What is the precise plan? What is the next step?
Am I accurate?
What does the evidence show?
Can I support my idea with numbers?

"A great many people think they are thinking when they are merely rearranging their prejudices."

—William James

Description: Your Inner Healthy Skeptic

If you prefer the Thinking style, you are probably known for your disciplined involvement in abstract and logical reasoning. You like to remove yourself from the bias of emotions and specific situations. In fact, you probably prefer to work alone. This allows you to make predictable, dependable plans and look for weaknesses and inconsistencies in other's work. You may be described as skeptical, structured, linear, and controlled. You can detect a problem a mile away.

You may prefer to approach your personal development by understanding the concept behind the change you're trying to make. This helps you be committed to taking the emotional risk of leaving your comfort zone.

Overusing the Thinking Style

If you overuse the Thinking style, you probably dread the word "emotional." You may devalue the importance of emotions and relationships and avoiding working with other people. This can make you seem cold or lost in thought. You may also find yourself latching on to one idea without keeping an open mind.

Using the Thinking Style to Lead a Team

The strength of the Thinking style is a balance between neutrality and precision. When you are leading a group process, maintain your conviction and use data to support your approach. As your team members progress in their work, calmly override emotional outbursts with a neutral position. Review all the team members' ideas and concerns in a logical analysis. Bring accuracy, high quality, and thoroughness to the team's process and outcome.

Communicating in the Thinking Style

When you want to communicate in the Thinking style or communicate with someone who prefers the Thinking style, begin by focusing on a logical progression of facts. Strive to back up your claims with numbers. Focus on facts and issues, make a thorough spreadsheet, and discuss costs and benefits.

Address conflict by focusing on facts and figures and being prepared for skepticism. Defuse tension by stepping back, being objective and logical, and downplaying emotions.

Key Phrases

"Where are the numbers that prove this point?"

"I see a problem here."

"What evidence do you have?"

Here is a typical e-mail communication using the Thinking style:

Subject: Tomorrow's meeting

Message: Meet in the conference room at 12 to discuss new client approach.

Budget attached.

Flexing to the Thinking Style

In the Thinking style, you can learn to generalize information through the use of concepts. You become able to think in a disciplined, logical way and give clear directions. Rather than let emotions cloud your thoughts, you learn to distance yourself and remain neutral. You can use this neutrality as a foundation for developing experiments that yield hard data.

You should flex to the Thinking style when you want to make rational decisions, conduct experiments, analyze and manipulate quantitative data, or be consistent and accurate. To begin flexing to the Thinking style, you can embody the physical characteristics of the style, practice exercises that draw your attention to the capabilities of the style, or ask yourself key questions that will help remind you of how to use the style effectively. Use your body to help you flex to the Thinking style:

Narrow your vision to the task at hand.

Turn your body toward your work.

Be thorough and accurate in your movements.

Use these techniques to begin flexing to the Thinking style:

Listen to a newscast and identify the way the newscaster uses implication and innuendo instead of facts.

Engage in a political discussion in an election year and remain detached.

Conduct a cost-to-benefit analysis.

Deciding

Capabilities

Finding practical solutions to problems
Committing to a goal
Making decisions and solving problems
Taking a stand, even on controversial issues

Preferred Environments

Orderly, uncluttered spaces
Efficient, ergonomically designed spaces
Environments conducive to completing projects

Stressors

Being in ambiguous situations
Dealing with indecisive people
Losing control
Facing unclear expectations
Being unable to complete tasks

Key Questions

Can I make small comparisons?
How will I know if I have reached my goal?
What is the low-hanging fruit?
What is the most practical approach?
What is the bottom line?
How can I focus on one course of action?

"Language is never neutral."

—*Paulo Freire*

Description: Your Inner Judge

If you prefer the Deciding style, you take risks to identify the best option of many, confident that you have considered the available facts. You focus, commit, measure progress toward goals, and drive efficiency. You determine standards and criteria for success so that you can measure whether or not you make it to the finish line. If progress does not go as planned, you seek critical feedback so that you can make positive adjustments.

You may prefer to approach personal development with a specific goal in mind. Once you commit to change, you will measure your progress toward attaining that goal.

Overusing the Deciding Style

If you overuse the Deciding style, you probably dread the word "brainstorm." You avoid dealing with ambiguity and lack of focus. You can become obsessed with goal achievement and efficiency, making you seem judgmental and impatient. You may also find yourself missing opportunities by clinging to one course of action.

Using the Deciding Style to Lead a Team

The strength of the Deciding style is a focus on the finish line, with practical results and well-defined success. When you are leading a group process, respect hierarchy and organizational structure. As your team members progress in their work, help them base decisions on data, and then fiercely guide them through following up. Commit to a plan, clarify the goal, and balance efficiency and effectiveness.

Communicating in the Deciding Style

When you want to communicate in the Deciding style or communicate with someone who prefers the Deciding style, begin by using language that is clear, pragmatic, direct, and efficient. Take a practical approach, measure success, and provide critical feedback. Focus on best practices. Address conflict clearly and directly, making efficient use of time. Defuse tension by setting clear standards of success and focusing on how to reach a mutual goal.

Key Phrases

"Here's our goal."

"How will we know if we succeed?"

"Take this direction."

Here is a typical e-mail communication using the Deciding style:

Subject: Tomorrow's meeting at 1p.m.

Message: I want to make certain that our meeting is productive. Please be clear about the goals and expectations for the session. We need to be able to determine the associated costs to get the job done efficiently.

Flexing to the Deciding Style

In the Deciding style, you can learn to focus on solving problems to reach practical outcomes. You become able to commit to one path toward reaching one goal. This commitment helps you adopt an attitude that is realistic, accountable, and direct.

You should flex to the Deciding style when you want to solve problems, commit to a goal or clear intention, make a strong impact, or focus on practical outcomes. To begin flexing to the Deciding style, you can embody the physical characteristics of the style, practice exercises that draw your attention to the capabilities of the style, or ask yourself key questions that will help remind you of how to use the style effectively.

Use your body to help you flex to the Deciding style:

Focus on feeling strong and grounded.

Be firm, intentional, and perhaps even abrupt with your movements.

Use these techniques to begin flexing to the Deciding style:

Set a goal and determine how you will measure success.

Avoid procrastination and perfectionism, the enemies of decision making.

Watch videos of referees in action and notice how firmly they commit.

Acting

Capabilities

Meeting time deadlines
Finding ways to make things happen
Taking goal-oriented action to achieve results
Implementing plans with limited resources

Preferred Environments

Dynamic environments
Work environments that reward achievement

Stressors

Waiting
Focusing on the process without clear outcomes
Being delayed by perfectionism
Being unable to complete tasks

Key Questions

Are my actions purposeful and efficient?
What small action can I take now?
How can I engage with the environment?
Am I holding myself back?
Am I completing my checklist?
How can I keep things moving?

"The self is not something ready-made, but something in continuous formation through choice of action."

—John Dewey

Description: Your Inner Achiever

If you prefer the Acting style, you take assertive, goal-directed steps to get things done. You implement, execute, coordinate, and drive toward the finish line. With this style, you are adept at leading teams because you care about completing tasks and meeting people's needs. You are on time, achievement-oriented, and fearless. You have a checklist going all the time. Your assertive attitude is dynamic and commanding—you just want to do it and do it now! You can always try again. Who cares if you make a little mistake? You may just get it right the first time—and you will be ahead of the game if you do.

You may prefer to approach your personal development by trying new things whenever you have an opportunity.

Overusing the Acting Style

If you overuse the Acting style, you probably dread the word "wait." You often take risks to be successful, even if you sometimes aim at the wrong target or solve the wrong problem. You are prone to panicking, acting prematurely, or being busy without achieving actual results.

Using the Acting Style to Lead a Team

The strength of the Acting style is the ability to move constantly toward a goal. When you are leading a group process, balance the needs of your team members with the need to get things done. As your team members progress in their work, keep sessions short to allow maximum time for getting things done.

Communicating in the Acting Style

When you want to communicate in the Acting style or communicate with someone who prefers the Acting style, begin by speaking dynamically and rapidly, in a commanding tone. Focus on checklists and the urgency to complete them. Return phone calls immediately. Address conflict by showing concern for people and issues while focusing on getting things done quickly. Defuse tension by taking a walk with the people involved in the dispute. Do something that moves toward resolution. Allow people to voice their feelings, and do not take it personally.

Key Phrases

"Let's do this!"

"Who does what by when?"

"What one action can we take right now?"

"Time is money."

Here is a typical e-mail communication using the Acting style:

Subject: Tomorrow's meeting

Message: We have a quick turnaround time on the decisions that we must make tomorrow. Here is a checklist of the items we expect from you. Come early for lunch—the meeting will begin precisely at noon.

Flexing to the Acting Style

In the Acting style, you can learn to implement plans and get things done. You become able to seize the moment to accomplish goals, even when you need to experiment with a trial-and-error approach. Rather than fixate on developing a perfect strategy, you learn to act quickly in urgent situations.

You should flex to the Acting style when you want to make a change, accomplish goals, and take risks. To begin flexing to the Acting style, you can embody the physical characteristics of the style, practice exercises that draw your attention to the capabilities of the style, or ask yourself key questions that will help remind you of how to use the style effectively.

Use your body to help you flex to the Acting style

Use an assertive, dynamic, and commanding tone.

Be alert and ready to act at a moment's notice.

Move quickly and confidently with strong but fluid motions.

Use these techniques to begin flexing to the Acting style:

Make a to-do list and check things off.

Practice doing something more quickly than you typically do just for a short time: walking, getting dressed, or talking. Notice how differently you feel.

Ask a question when you do not know what to do. Speaking is a form of action.

Initiating

Capabilities

Flexibly adapting to changing contexts and conditions
Influencing and motivating others
Recognizing new opportunities
Bouncing back from failure

Preferred Environments

Dynamic, real-life situations
Environments with networking opportunities
Spaces conducive to completing projects

Stressors

Facing ambiguity and indecisiveness
Losing control or clarity
Being alone for too long
Being unable to complete tasks

Key Questions

What action would I take if I had no fear?
How can I use humor?
How can I best relate to the people around me?
What is at the edge that I may not notice?
How can I curb my inhibitions in the moment?

> *"Arriving at one goal is the starting point to another."*
>
> *—John Dewey*

Description: Your Inner Influencer

If you prefer the Initiating style, you probably prefer starting things rather than getting caught in the thick of the details, but you can influence others to do that for you. You thrive in a fast-paced, dynamic environment. This allows you to focus on many things in rapid succession, remaining innately optimistic about all the possibilities. You thrive on social interactions and your networking skills, and others may call you outgoing, energetic, or courageous. You are proud of your accomplishments and never shy away from the limelight. In the Initiating style, you are able to shrug off losses or "failure" in favor of trying again.

You may prefer to approach your personal development using trial and error whenever an exciting opportunity presents itself.

Overusing the Initiating Style

If you overuse the Initiating style, you probably dread the words "status quo." You sometimes have trouble listening to others and can be perceived as impulsive, pushy, or impatient. You may find yourself needing to be in the spotlight and acting carelessly or illogically—like a whirlwind.

Using the Initiating Style to Lead a Team

The strength of the Initiating style is being able to take decisive action in a changing environment. When you are leading a group process, use your gut instinct and persuade others to follow your lead by communicating the need for urgency. As your team members progress in their work, you can keep things moving along without excessive deliberation.

Communicating in the Initiating Style

When you want to communicate in the Initiating style or communicate with someone who prefers the Initiating style, begin by using inspiring, energetic language. Set the pace, seize the opportunity, and grab the prize. Make connections and introductions while being improvisational and persuasive. Address conflict after showing optimism, enthusiasm, and nonjudgmental humor. Defuse tension by facing situations quickly and directly, remaining open to change, and expecting spontaneity and rapid-fire questions.

Key Phrases

"Let's go with it."

"Don't miss out."

"You can do this."

Here is a typical e-mail communication using the Initiating style:

Subject: Way to go

Message: Great job—on time and on budget! Lunch is on me tomorrow. Now, let's move on to our next opportunity. Comment on the attached agenda ASAP.

Flexing to the Initiating Style

In the Initiating style, you can learn to seize opportunities by jumping right in without deliberating. You become able to push forward in the face of challenge, improvise to keep moving forward, and bounce back in the event of failure. This ability helps you think quickly, act on a hunch, and take risks while using your powers of persuasion to enlist others to join your cause.

You should flex to the Initiating style when you want to influence or take the lead, act on new opportunities, think in the moment, and manage high-energy situations. To begin flexing to the Initiating style, you can embody the physical characteristics of the style, practice exercises that draw your attention to the capabilities of the style, or ask yourself key questions that will help remind you of how to use the style effectively.

Use your body to help you flex to the Initiating style:

Use exuberant, spontaneous movements.

Be ready to seize new opportunities in an instant.

Focus on self-confidence, fluidity, and mobility.

Use these techniques to begin flexing to the Initiating style:

Try improvisation by beginning each sentence with "Yes, and."

Make three positive statements for every negative statement.

When feeling afraid, count to ten so your "thinking brain" can come to your aid.

Balancing

Capabilities

Identifying the blind sports in a whole situation
Bridging differences between people
Adapting to shifting priorities
Displaying resourcefulness

Preferred Environments

Quiet, organized, solitary environments when using
 the
Reflecting, Analyzing, Thinking, and Deciding styles
Dynamic, social, stimulating environments when using
 the Experiencing, Imagining, Acting, and Initiating
 styles

Stressors

Facing ambiguity and indecisiveness
Needing to specialize
Needing to take a strong stance in any one style

Remaining committed to one style throughout a situation

Key Questions

Have I considered all possibilities, weighed all options?
Is there a blind spot?
Do we need to change our approach?
Have I filled in the gaps?
Am I accommodating and adapting?

"So be sure when you step, step with care and great tact. And remember that life's A Great Balancing Act."

—Dr. Seuss

Description: Your Inner Adapter

If you prefer the Balancing style, you adapt by moving between acting, reflecting, feeling, and thinking as the situation demands. Although you may still have preferences for other learning styles, you are able to change your approach to match the context. You see the value of all the learning styles. Therefore, you may be able to help others take a particular perspective and fill in gaps as needed. It can be a little confusing at times since you are rooted in a style that is more flexible than stable.

Overusing the Balancing Style

If you overuse the Balancing style, you probably dread the word "commit." You may risk becoming a chameleon that adapts dutifully to the situation at hand, which can be confusing both for you and for the people you interact with. You may find yourself unable to sustain commitment or hold to your opinion, frequently changing your mind and direction.

Using the Balancing Style to Lead a Team

The strength of the Balancing style is the ability to bridge differences and identify blind spots. When you are leading a group process, change your approach based upon the context. As your team members progress in their work, involve each of them and empower them to contribute their ideas. Fill in the gaps by identifying parts of the learning cycle that might be missing from the team's process.

Communicating in the Balancing Style

When you want to communicate in the Balancing style or communicate with someone who prefers the Balancing style, focus on remaining flexible. Use verbal and nonverbal communication in a way that reflects how a situation might be changing, and strive for a holistic perspective. Address conflict by being appreciative, cheerful, and adaptable. Defuse tension by allowing other people involved to identify options and blind spots and collaborating to share a solution.

Key Phrases

"On one hand ... yet, on the other hand,..."

"We have a blind spot."

Here is a typical e-mail communication using the Balancing style:

Subject: Tomorrow's meeting

Message: If you cannot make the meeting tomorrow, please let me know. We have lots of moving pieces to this project, so we want to detect any blind spots before we make decisions.

Flexing to the Balancing Style

In the Balancing style, you learn to wear many hats, weigh different options, and change your approach based on the situation. You can become a jack-of-all-trades, master of none. Rather than cling to one learning style, you learn to fluidly use the style that is called for or the one that is missing from the process. This fluidity helps you fit in everywhere.

You should flex to the Balancing style when you want to adapt to a new or changing situation or work with diverse people. To begin flexing to the Balancing style, you can embody the physical characteristics of the style, practice exercises that draw your attention to the capabilities of the style, or ask yourself key questions that will help remind you of how to use the style effectively.

Use your body to help you flex to the Balancing style:

> Practice jumping between calm, relaxed states and alert, reactive states.

> Practice alternating between still, tense motions and open, fluid motions.

Use these techniques to begin flexing to the Balancing style:

> Practice being a "chameleon" by adapting your clothing, level of formality, body language, and communication style to match the group you are joining.

> Attend a function you would not normally attend and notice the ways you adapt.

> Read an article and identify all the missing perspectives.

About the Authors

Kay Peterson

Kay Peterson is the founder of the Institute for Experiential Learning, an organization dedicated to promoting the understanding and practice of Experiential Learning, and a founder and the Co-CEO of Harlan Peterson Partners, an organization development and executive coaching firm. Kay applies Experiential Learning to develop leaders, drive team effectiveness, and promote learning organizations. Through an executive coaching program that builds learning flexibility, Kay inspires professionals across industries and at all stages in their careers to achieve their highest potential. She has consulted with professionals and organizations in health care, law, service, finance, manufacturing, management, engineering, IT, education, and nonprofit settings. Together with David Kolb, Kay is developing a Learning Skills Profile 360° Assessment that promotes personal and professional development by measuring skills associated with the Learning Styles of the Kolb Learning Style Inventory 4.0.

Kay earned a BS from Vanderbilt University, an MS-POD and a MBA from Case Western Reserve University. In addition, she holds an MN from Emory University and has pursued postgraduate training at the Gestalt Institute of Cleveland in gestalt coaching (Gestalt Professional Certified Coach), gestalt training, and somatic studies. Her work in experiential learning has been published in *HBR Guides, OD Practitioner,* and the *Journal of Experiential Learning.* For more information, go to www.experientiallearninginstitute.org and www.harlanpeterson.com.

David A. Kolb

David Kolb is the chairman of Experience Based Learning Systems (EBLS), an organization that he founded in 1980 to advance research and practice on experiential learning. EBLS has developed many experiential exercises and self-assessment instruments, including the latest Kolb Learning Style Inventory 4.0 and the Kolb Educator Role Profile, an inventory designed to help educators apply experiential learning principles in their work.

David Kolb received his BA in psychology, philosophy, and religion at Knox College and his PhD in social psychology from Harvard University. He was a professor of organizational behavior and management at the MIT Sloan School of Management and at the Weatherhead School of Management, Case Western Reserve University, where he is currently Emeritus Professor of Organizational Behavior.

He is best known for his research on experiential learning and learning styles described in the new second edition of *Experiential Learning: Experience as the Source of Learning and Development.* Other books include *Conversational Learning: An Experiential Approach to Knowledge Creation, Innovation in Professional Education: Steps on a Journey from Teaching to Learning,* and *Organizational Behavior: An Experiential Approach.* In addition he has authored many journal articles and book chapters on experiential learning. David has received several research awards and four honorary degrees recognizing his contributions to experiential learning in higher education. For more information about his work, go to www.learningfrome xperience.com

Berrett–Koehler
BK Publishers

Berrett-Koehler is an independent publisher dedicated to an ambitious mission: *Connecting people and ideas to create a world that works for all.*

We believe that the solutions to the world's problems will come from all of us, working at all levels: in our organizations, in our society, and in our own lives. Our BK Business books help people make their organizations more humane, democratic, diverse, and effective (we don't think there's any contradiction there). Our BK Currents books offer pathways to creating a more just, equitable, and sustainable society. Our BK Life books help people create positive change in their lives and align their personal practices with their aspirations for a better world.

All of our books are designed to bring people seeking positive change together around the ideas that empower them to see and shape the world in a new way.

And we strive to practice what we preach. At the core of our approach is Stewardship, a deep sense of responsibility to administer the company for the benefit of all of our stakeholder groups including authors, customers, employees, investors, service providers, and the communities and environment around us. Everything we do is built around this and our other key values of quality, partnership, inclusion, and sustainability.

This is why we are both a B-Corporation and a California Benefit Corporation—a certification and a for-profit legal status that require us to adhere to the highest standards for corporate, social, and environmental performance.

We are grateful to our readers, authors, and other friends of the company who consider themselves to be part of the BK Community. We hope that you, too, will join us in our mission.

A BK Business Book

We hope you enjoy this BK Business book. BK Business books pioneer new leadership and management practices and socially responsible approaches to business. They are designed to provide you with groundbreaking and practical tools to transform your work and organizations while upholding the triple bottom line of people, planet, and profits. High-five!

To find out more, visit www.bkconnection.com.

Berrett–Koehler
Publishers

Connecting people and ideas
to create a world that works for all

Dear Reader,

Thank you for picking up this book and joining our worldwide community of Berrett-Koehler readers. We share ideas that bring positive change into people's lives, organizations, and society.

To welcome you, we'd like to offer you a free e-book. You can pick from among twelve of our bestselling books by entering the promotional code **BKP92E** here: http://www.bkconnection.com/welcome.

When you claim your free e-book, we'll also send you a copy of our e-newsletter, the *BK Communiqué.* Although you're free to unsubscribe, there are many benefits to sticking around. In every issue of our newsletter you'll find

- A free e-book

- Tips from famous authors

- Discounts on spotlight titles

- Hilarious insider publishing news

- A chance to win a prize for answering a riddle

Best of all, our readers tell us, "Your newsletter is the only one I actually read." So claim your gift today, and please stay in touch!

Sincerely,

Charlotte Ashlock
Steward of the BK Website

Questions? Comments? Contact me at bkcommunity@ bkpub.com.

Certified
B
Corporation
bcorporation.net

A

Abstract conceptualization and abstract thinking, *21*

Abstract thinking and experiential learning cycle, *21, 22*

Acting style,
  communication preferences by learning style, *67*
  definition, *53*
  developing capacity for, *106*

Active experimentation and experiential learning cycle, *21, 22*

Adaptation, learning style and life path, *58*

Adult development theories, *9*

Affinity for others and learning style, *65, 66*

Analyzing style,
  communication preferences by learning style, *67*

definition, *50, 51*
developing capacity for, *105*

Application of knowledge of learning styles, *81*
  automaticity, *81*
  entrenchment, *81*
  flexibility, *81*
  framework for development, *81*
  success and, *81*

Approach to life, *117, 118, 119, 120, 122, 123, 124, 125, 127, 128, 129, 130, 132, 133, 134, 135, 136, 137*
  beginning of career, perfecting skills at, *119, 120*
  expression of total self, *132, 133, 134*
  later career and learning to develop, *122, 123, 124, 125*
  purpose, *134, 135, 136*
  specialization in career, *120, 122*
  transitions and career change, *125, 127, 128*
  well-worn pathways, *118, 119*

240

Art of Changing the Brain, The: Enriching Teaching by Exploring the Biology of Learning (Zull), *22, 23*

Attachment to style, *102*

Attachment to style as limitation to flexibility, *94*

Automatic engagement, *4*

Automaticity and application of knowledge of learning styles, *81*

Automatic pilot vs. paying attention with high performance teams, *78*

Autopoesis, *8*

Awareness, *89*

B

Backup learning style concept, *92, 100*

Balancing style,
  communication preferences by learning style, *67*
  definition, *57*
  developing capacity for, *106*

Beginning of career, perfecting skills at, *119, 120*

Being witness of our own process, *144, 145*

Body sensations and reactions and intentional attention, *141*

Breathing and mindfulness, *140, 141*

Bridges, William, *125, 127*

Bridging communication gaps and learning style, *67*

Buddhist meditation and mindfulness, *140*

Buddhist practice and focusing, *143*

C

Campbell, Neve, *12*

Career and learning way, *119, 120, 122, 123, 124, 125, 127, 128*
  beginning of career, perfecting skills at, *119, 120*
  later career and learning to develop, *122, 123*
  mid-career, complexlty in, *120, 122*
  specialization in career, *120, 122, 123, 124, 125*
  transitions and career change, *125, 127*

Career choice, learning style and life path, *59, 61*

Caring and purpose, *134*

Challenging yourself, *111*

freedom and confidence development, *111*

self-development goal, *111*

Choosing style to match situation, *144*

Client development example, learning cycle use for life of learning, *28, 30, 31*

Cognitive neuroscience, *23*

Comfort zone, *102*

Communication differences and learning style, *66*

Acting style, *67*

Analyzing style, *67*

Balancing style, *67*

Deciding style, *67*

Experiencing style, *67*

Imagining style, *67*

Initiating style, *67*

Reflecting style, *67*

Thinking style, *67*

Concrete experience and experiential learning cycle, *21, 22*

Conflict and flexibility and expression of total self, *132*

Connecting with alternate style upside, *103*

Creation of self by learning, *6, 8*

learning from experience spiral, *8*

self-creation and learning, *8*

D

Dane, Erik, *129*

Day-to-day problem solving guide, learning cycle use, *26*

Deciding style, communication preferences by learning style, *67*

definition, *52, 53*

developing capacity for, *105, 106*

Decision-making example, learning cycle use for life of learning, *27*

Deep experiencing practice, *140, 141, 143, 144*

experiencing vs. experience as source of learning, *140*

focusing, *143, 144*

intentional attention, *141*

mindfulness, *140, 141*

Deliberate learning for life, *139, 140, 141, 143, 144, 145, 146, 147, 149, 150, 151, 152, 154, 156* deep experiencing practice, *140, 141, 143, 144*

learning process and deliberateness, *144, 145, 146*

start small with one big thing, *146, 147, 149, 150, 151, 152*

Deliberate use of multiple styles with high performance teams, *76*

Dewey, John, *10, 140*

Difficulties in developing learning flexibility, *102, 103, 104*

attachment, *102*

connecting with alternate style upside, *103*

inertia, *102*

overtoleration of downside of preferred style, *102*

Diversity with high performance teams, *74*

Dominant learning style concept, *92, 100*

Dweck, Carol, *12*

E

Edison, Thomas, *151*

Embodiment of style, *109, 111*

movement preferences, *111*

physical flexibility, *109*

Embracing of learning identity, *15, 16*

fixed self and identity, *16*

mastery response and identity, *16*

Empathy, *10, 134*

Ending stage in career transition, *127*

Engrained habits, *61*

Entrenchment and application of knowledge of learning styles, *81*

Ericsson, K. Anders, *149*

Ethical practices and purpose, *135*

Experience and decision making, *5*

Experience and flexibility building, *100, 102*

awareness, *100*

backup style, *100*

comfort zone, *100*

dominant style, *100*

self-direction, *102*

Experience and remembered thinking self, *6*

Experience as gateway to learning, *4, 5, 6*

automatic engagement, *4*

experience and decision making, *5*

experience and remembered thinking self, *6*

remembered thinking self, *6*

Theraveda Buddhism, *4*

Experiencing self as a process, *132*

Experiencing self as subject vs. object, *133*

Experiencing style,
  communication preferences by learning style, *67*
  definition, *47, 48*
  developing capacity for, *104*

Experiencing vs. experience as source of learning, *140*

Experiential learning and brain structure, *23*

Experiential learning cycle, *19, 20, 21*
  abstract thinking, *20*
  active experimentation, *20*
  concrete experience, *20*
  reflective observation, *20*

Expert performance research, *149*

Expression of total self, *132, 133, 134*
  conflict and flexibility, *130, 132*
  experiencing self as a process, *132*
  experiencing self as subject vs. object, *133*
  interdependence and independence, *133, 134*

Extroversion, *41*

F

Feedback preferences and learning style, *67*

Felt sense and focusing, *144*

Fit of style vs. limitations of fit, *94, 96*

Fixed self and identity, *16*

Flexibility and application of knowledge of learning styles, *81*

Flexibility in style, building, *86, 87, 89, 92, 93, 94, 96, 97, 99, 100, 102, 103, 104, 105, 106, 109, 111, 113, 115*
  Anne Robinson story, *87, 89*
  backup learning style concept, *92*

challenging yourself, *111*
difficulties in developing learning flexibility, *102, 103, 104, 105, 106*
dominant learning style concept, *92*
embodiment of style, *109, 111*
experience and flexibility building, *100, 102*
flexing style for multiple activities, *93, 94*
freedom and confidence and, *92*
learning, *86, 87, 89, 92, 93, 94*
matching situations with flexibility, *93, 94, 96, 97, 99, 100*
Flexing style for multiple activities, *105*
Flow concept, *146*
Focusing, *143, 144*
Buddhist practice, *143*
felt sense, *144*
safe and quiet space, *143*
Focusing (Gendlin), *143*
Foundation of developmental process and specialization in career, *120*

Framework for development and application of capacities, *104, 105, 106*
Acting, *106*
Analyzing, *105*
Balancing, *106*
Deciding, *105, 106*
Experiencing, *104*
Imagining, *104, 105*
Initiating, *106*
Reflecting, *105*
Thinking, *105*
Framework for development and application of knowledge of learning styles, *81*
Freedom and confidence, development from challenging yourself, *111*
from flexibility, *92*
Freire, Paulo, *15*
Full-cycle learners, *136*

G

Gandhi, Mahatma, *117*
Gendlin, Eugene, *143*
Generativity and purpose, *135*
Graham, Martha, *139*

Grocery shopping example, learning cycle use for life of learning, *31, 32*

H

Heinlein, Robert, *117*
Horton, Myles, *58, 59*
Humility and learning, *11*
    mastery and competence, *11*
    openness to experience, *11*

I

Identification of learning style preferences with high performance teams, *75*
Imagining style,
    communication preferences by learning style, *67*
    definition, *48, 49*
    developing capacity for, *104, 105*
Impact of learning style and choices on life, *63, 64, 65*
Implementation of starting small with one big thing, *152*
Inclusion of missing steps with high performance teams, *78*

Inertia and difficulties in developing learning flexibility, *102*
Initiating style,
    communication preferences by learning style, *67*
    definition, *56*
    developing capacity for, *106*
Innate sense of morality, *10*
In-process nature of styles vs. static trait, *42*
Integrated flexible approach in later career and learning to develop, *122, 123*
Intentional attention, *141*
    body sensations and reactions, *141*
    self-creation through learning, *141*
Interdependence and, independence and expression of total self, *133, 134*
Introversion, *41*

K

Kabat-Zinn, Jon, *140*
Kahneman, Daniel, *4*

KLSI 4.0 learning styles, *47, 48, 49, 50, 51, 52, 53, 54, 56, 57*
  Acting style, *53, 54*
  Analyzing style, *50, 51*
  Balancing style, *57*
  Deciding style, *52, 53*
  Experiencing style, *47, 48*
  Imagining style, *48, 49*
  Initiating style, *56*
  Reflecting style, *49, 50*
  Thinking style, *51, 52*
Kolb Learning Style Inventory 4.0, *42, 43*
  background, *42*

L

Later career and learning to develop, *122, 123, 124, 125*
  integrated flexible approach, *123*
  map for professional growth, *123*
  path of integration, *123, 124*
Leadership development program example, learning cycle use for life of learning, *33*
Learner, being, *15, 16, 17, 19, 20, 21, 22, 23, 25, 26, 27, 28, 30, 31, 32, 33, 36, 37, 38*
  automaticity, *14*

  embracing of learning identity, *15, 16*
  fixed identity, *12*
  learning cycle use for life of learning, *26, 27, 28, 30, 31, 32, 33*
  learning how to learn, *16, 17, 19, 20, 21, 22, 23, 25, 26*
Learning cycle use and life path, *41, 42*
  extroversion, *41*
  in-process nature of styles vs. static trait, *42*
  introversion, *41*
Learning cycle use for life of learning, *26, 27, 28, 30, 31, 32, 33*
  client development example, *28, 30, 31*
  as day-to-day problem-solving guide, *26*
  decision-making example, *27*
  grocery-shopping example, *31, 32*
  leadership development program example, *33*
Learning from experience spiral, *8*
Learning life force, *8, 9*
  adult development theories, *9*

autopoesis, *8*
self-actualization, *9*
self-authorship, *9*
Learning how to learn, *16, 17, 19, 20, 21, 22, 23, 25, 26*
cognitive neuroscience, *23*
experiential learning and brain structure, *23*
experiential learning cycle, *19, 20, 21, 22*
full-cycle learners, *22*
memory for names, *17*
Learning process and deliberateness, *144, 145, 146*
choosing style to match situation, *144*
flow concept, *146*
10,000-hour rule, *146*
as witness of own process, *144, 145*
Learning style and approach to life, *61, 62, 63, 64*
engrained habits, *61*
impact of choices on life, *63, 64, 65*
way of being in the world, *61, 62, 63*
Learning style and life path, *58, 59, 61*
adaptation, *58*
and career choice, *58, 59, 61*

Learning style and understanding others, *62, 63, 64*
affinity for others, *65, 66*
bridging communication gaps, *67*
communication differences, *66*
communication preferences by learning style, *67*
feedback preferences, *67*
timing and tone, *66*
Learning style awareness, use of, *8*
Learning styles and learning cycle connection, *72*
Learning styles with high, performance teams: nursing, *74, 75, 76, 78, 79*
automatic pilot vs. paying attention, *78*
deliberate use of multiple styles, *76*
diversity, *74*
identification of learning style preferences, *75*
inclusion of skipped steps, *78*
missing steps, *75*

process guide, *76*
shared leadership, *79*
skipped steps, *75*
synergy, *74*
task vs. relationship, *74*
Learning way, *2, 3, 4, 5, 6, 8, 9, 10*
creation of self by learning, *6, 8*
experience as gateway to learning, *4, 5, 6*
humility and learning, *11*
learning life force, *8, 9*
moral purpose, life of, *10*
process of learning, *3*
Leonard, George, *150*
Life path and learning style, *40, 41, 42, 43, 47, 48, 49, 50, 51, 52, 53, 54, 56, 57, 58, 59, 61, 62, 63, 64, 65, 66, 67, 72, 74, 75, 76, 78, 79, 81, 82, 84*
application of knowledge of learning styles, *81*
KLSI 4.0 learning styles, *47, 48, 49, 50, 51, 52, 53, 54, 56, 57, 58*
Kolb Learning Style Inventory 4.0, *43*
learning cycle use, *41, 42*
learning style and approach to life, *61, 62, 63, 64, 65*
learning style and life path, *58, 59*

learning style awareness, use of, *65*
learning styles and learning cycle connection, *72, 74*
learning styles with high performance teams: nursing, *74, 75, 76, 78, 79*

M
Mastery (Leonard), *150*
Mastery and competence, *11*
Mastery response and identity, *16*
Matching situations with flexibility, *94, 96, 97, 99, 100*
attachment to style, *94*
fit vs. limitations, *96*
nondominant style experimentation, *99*
overuse of preferred style, limiting, *96, 97*
situational use of learning style, *99*
Map for professional growth in later career and learning to develop, *123*
Maslow, Abraham, *9*
Maturana, Humberto, *8*
Memory for names, *17*

Mid-career, complexity in and specialization in career, *120, 122*

Mindfulness, *140, 141*
   breathing, *141*
   Buddhist meditation, *140*
   sensory awareness, *141*

Missing steps with highperformance teams, *75*

Moral purpose, life of, *10*
   empathy, *10*
   innate sense of morality, *10*

Movement preferences as embodiment of style, *111*

N
Neutral zone in career transition, *127*

New beginning stage in career transition, *128*
   backup learning style concept, *92*
   dominant learning style concept, *92*
   flexing style for multiple activities, *93*
   freedom and confidence and, *92*

Nondominant style,

experimentation to match situations with flexibility, *99*

O
Openness to experience, *10*

Overtoleration of downside of preferred style, difficulties in developing learning flexibility, *102*

Overuse of preferred style and limitations, *96, 97*

P
Path of integration in later career and learning to develop, *123, 124*

Paying attention to process vs. outcome, *149, 150*

Physical flexibility to embody style, *109*

Playing to strengths of well-worn pathways, *118*

Practice for the sake of practice, *150*

Process guide with high performance teams, *76*

Process of learning vs. learning content and specialization in career, *122*

Purpose, *134, 135, 136*

250

caring, *134*
empathy, *134*
ethical practices, *135*
generativity, *135*
quality, *134*

Q
Quality and purpose, *134*

R
Redefining failure, *151*
Reflecting style,
 communication
 preferences by learning
 style, *67*
 definition, *49, 50*
 developing capacity for,
 105
Reflective observation and
experiential learning cycle,
20
Reinforcement of well-worn
pathways, *118, 119*
Remembered thinking self,
6
Risk, *152*
Robinson, Anne, *87, 89*
Rogers, Carl, *6, 10, 143*

S
Safe and quiet space and
focusing, *143*

Self-actualization, *9*
Self-authorship, *9*
Self-creation and learning,
8
Self-creation through
learning, *141*
Self-development goal to
challenge yourself, *111*
Self-direction, *102*
Sensory awareness and
mindfulness, *141*
Shared leadership with high
performance teams, *79*
Situational use of learning
style, *99*
Skipped steps with high
performance teams, *75, 78*
Specialization in career, *120,
122*
 foundation of
 developmental process,
 120
 mid-career, complexity
 in, *122*
 process of learning vs.
 learning content, *122*
Start small with one big
thing, *146, 147, 149, 150, 151, 152*
 expert performance
 research, *149*
 implementation, *152*

paying attention to process vs. outcome, *149, 150*

practice for the sake of practice, *150*

redefine failure, *151*

risk, *152*

time frame establishment, *149*

trust of learning process, *150, 151*

Success and application of knowledge of learning styles, *81*

Synergy with high performance teams, *74*

T

Task vs. relationship with high performance teams, *74*

10,000 hour rule, *146*

Theraveda Buddhism, *4*

Thinking style,
communication preferences by learning style, *67*
definition, *51, 52*
developing capacity for, *105*

Thoreau, Henry David, *86*

Time frame establishment of starting small with one big thing, *149*

Timing and tone and learning style, *66*

Transitions and career change, *125, 127, 128*
ending stage in career transition, *127*
neutral zone in career transition, *127*
new beginning stage in career transition, *128*

Trust of learning process of starting small with one big thing, *150, 151*

Twain, Mark, *3*

V

Varela, Francisco, *8*

W

Way of being in the world, learning style and, *61, 62, 63*

Weakest Link, The, *87, 89*

Well-worn pathways, *118, 119*
playing to strengths, *118*
reinforcement, *119*

Winfrey, Oprah, *3, 4*

Wolfe, Thomas, *2*

Work or life balance, *129, 130, 132*
  being present, *130*
  doubt-inducing
  exceptions to beliefs, *129*
  integration of multiple
  styles, *130, 132*

Z
Zull, James, *14, 22, 23*